RECOVERY

TRANSFORMING THE DESPAIR OF YOUR DIVORCE INTO AN UNEXPECTED GOOD

There is glorious life
ahead – (Really!)
Make it happen!

Suzy

RECOVERY

TRANSFORMING THE DESPAIR OF YOUR DIVORCE
INTO AN UNEXPECTED GOOD

SUZY BROWN

LEAFWOOD
PUBLISHERS

an imprint of Abilene Christian University Press

Radical Recovery

an imprint of Abilene Christian University Press

Copyright 2007 by Suzy Brown

ISBN 978-0-89112-518-1

Printed in the United States of America

Scripture quotations, unless otherwise noted, are from The Holy Bible,
New International Version. Copyright 1984, International Bible Society.
Used by permission of Zondervan Publishers.

Cover design by Nicole Weaver

For information contact:
Leafwood Publishers, Abilene, Texas
1-877-816-4455 toll free
www.leafwoodpublishers.com

To my family

With love and thanks to each of you
For being the precious gift you are.

"God is kind, but He's not soft.
In kindness, He takes us by the hand
and leads us to a radical life change."

Romans 2:4

The Message

CONTENTS

INTRODUCTION

I sat across the table from a beautiful, bright, accomplished, funny friend of mine. As we waited for our lunch, she began to talk. There was a little quiver in her voice, and her eyes were beginning to spill out tears. She said:

> I turned 50 in January. Our last child is leaving for college next year. I'm going through menopause, and I just found out my husband is having an affair with someone about twenty years younger than we are, and he wants out of our marriage. I'm losing everything all at once—and just when we were about to have a little breathing room—just when we were going to have more time for *us*. I've been raising children the last 25 years because that's what we wanted, and now the last one is getting ready to leave home. I haven't had a paying job since my husband was in medical school. My body is changing. My life is in complete turmoil. I can hardly get through the days, and the nights are worse. I've always been an optimist, but really— what am I going to do?

I know exactly how she feels. Stories like this have become much too personal and much too familiar. I had been living the same nightmare. I know what my friend is going through, and if you're reading this book, you are probably feeling those same devastating feelings.

In our small suburban neighborhood, there were four of us going through almost exactly the same situation, and we had a half dozen other close acquaintances in a similar storm as well. We had each been married at least 25 years. Almost all of us had struggled—most of the time, happily—through the early years of growing families and helping our husbands build their careers or professions. Now, just when things were beginning to calm down a little, slow down a little, all hell breaks loose.

My husband had a full-blown, three-year affair with a younger woman. He put absolutely everything at risk—his career, his family, even his relationship with his children. To try to explain it away as a midlife crisis is a cowardly cop-out. It is evidence of a devastating epidemic of self-centeredness, resulting in the destruction of long, good marriages and real flesh-and-blood families.

None of us were perfect wives. Our husbands weren't perfect husbands. We had marriages similar to most marriages with difficulties, baggage and two sides to every problem. We had good times and struggles. We had laughter and tears. But we all had strong, solid families with good—and in our opinions extraordinary—children who were maturing and making their way in the world. Some of us have grandchildren. But then, all of a sudden our husbands wanted a different life.

THE RADICAL WOMEN

Suddenly everywhere I turned, women were telling me their similar stories of betrayal and divorce. All of us were trying to cope the best we could on our own, but we needed help. So I started a small support group in an effort to make the trip through this emotional jungle easier for all of us. I decided on the name "Radical," meaning Rising Above Divorce In Confidence And Love.

We began to call ourselves the "Radical Women." The husband of each was having an affair with another woman. I was crushed when I found out about my husband, as was every other woman. And it wasn't only that each husband was having an affair—as devastating as that was—but that each was actually willing and eager to leave a relationship 25 or 30 or more years in the making.

If you are a Radical Woman, a woman going through a divorce, I'm sure the despair of that realization has set up camp somewhere in your life, too.

I asked a few of the women I knew who were going through a midlife divorce to meet every other week at my house. I put together a workbook to give some form to our first discussion. I was afraid we might all sit down around the table and just start crying and not be able to stop. I wanted some sort of agenda in hand to prevent that. As it happened, there were tears to be sure, but there was actually some laughing. My older brother jokingly said that he would call during the first meeting, and if the only thing he heard in the background was uncontrollable sobbing, he would send help.

The first Radical Recovery group met on shaky legs, and we began talking about the challenges we were facing. This book is the result of several years of those meetings, and it includes observations and input from everyone in the group. You are just getting our side of the story, of course. But if you're reading this, chances are you are going through a divorce, and our side is probably your side, too. None of us wanted to be divorced. But we had no choice. Together, we slowly began our process of Radical therapy and healing. We gained strength and courage and confidence from each other every time we met. We hope you will benefit from our journey, too.

The Radical Stage Names

Many years ago one of my book club friends mentioned an article she'd read about how to choose a name for the stage, or a new stage of life—especially if your new career of choice was to be an exotic dancer! Since then, I have known exactly what my stage name would be. The formula is simple: Your first name is the name of the first pet you remember, or your first doll, if you didn't have a pet. (My first dog's name was Frisky.) Your last name comes from the street where you lived in elementary school. (I lived at 920 North Ridgewood.) So, my name became Frisky Ridgewood. I love the name, actually, and think it could be a decent draw someday if my only option for buying groceries was to get a job at our local gentleman's club!

In some small way, giving ourselves stage names made us feel able to choose how to respond to this life-altering event. The names made us feel stronger and more alive at a time when we felt weak and defeated. Choosing a stage name was a way to show that we wouldn't let this situation destroy us—which was possible, unfortunately. We could use the stage names, if needed, to refer to ourselves or to write about ourselves incognito. And they were fun. Some women never get over a terrible divorce. Instead, we wanted to be more full of love and life on the other side of this trauma.

I know this divorce is not what you wanted. You never dreamed your life would unfold like this. You never thought you'd be here at this point in your life story. But the fact is, this is where you are. Accept that serious reality, and start the process of healing by taking one rebellious bit of control and figure out your own stage name—just in case you ever need it!

THE RADICAL MEETINGS & THE RADICAL BOOK

Committing to anything right now is hard. For me, committing to get together with other Radical Women was an important part of this journey. You can gain the insights of others through this book alone, or you can use this book to start your own Radical group. Identifying with other Radical Women either in person or through this book can be a great reassurance. It's encouraging to know that other women have survived what you are going through, and not only survived, but thrived! This book is designed for group discussion by chapter. Discussion questions are included at the book's end— either for group or personal reflection. Poems, to-do lists, and other material are included along the way as helps on your journey.

I know you've been crying a lot lately, and that's all the more reason for a good laugh now and then. All of us have done some pretty ridiculous things during this time of upheaval, and sharing those stories and laughing about them is very therapeutic. I'm not sure someone who has not been through a midlife divorce would fully appreciate or be able to really share in our sometimes bizarre humor. We laughed at both the ridiculous things we had done, and about the things we fantasized doing to our ex-husbands and to our ex-husbands' girlfriends. We never would have really done the things—I don't think!—but knowing that other Radical Women had thoughts like that, too, was a help. Healing begins by recognizing that there are things to laugh about—certainly we all know way too much about the tears. Reading about other women who have lived through all this is invaluable.

Our meetings were not "poor pitiful me!" gatherings. They were not pity parties or gripe and moan parties, bash the bum parties or victims anonymous meetings. They were Radical Recovery meetings. A Radical Recovery group that said, "Okay, this is horrendous, but what now?" It was an "I hate this, but how can I learn something good from this or help my children through this?" kind of group.

Early on it is hard to even talk to anyone about what's happening. I kept thinking my situation might be resolved before anyone found out. It's embarrassing and humiliating when your husband decides you're not quite fun enough or pretty enough or worth enough—and runs off with another woman (and in our opinion, a shameful excuse for a woman at that!). But when I talked with other women who had been going through the same thing, they knew. They understood how my heart was aching, how I thought I might not make it through the day (or night), why I kept thinking—hope against hope—that he would come to his senses.

Our goal has been that by sharing what we have learned, we can help ourselves and at the same time help other women get through the tragedy of a midlife divorce.

If you start your own Radical group, a good number of members is five to 12. Keep your ears open for women who are struggling. They will show up everywhere, I'm sad to say. Pick a safe, relaxed meeting place where feelings, however angry or sad or confused, can be expressed without fear or worry. Stick to soft drinks, bottled water, cider, coffee and tea and save anything stronger for other occasions! We need clear heads without any artificial stimulation making our erratic emotions even worse.

Set a time for the meeting to begin and end. Stay focused. Accept each woman where she is in the process. Don't get sidetracked into talking only about how terrible he was and how unfair it all is. We're looking for solutions. We can't do anything about the past, but we can grab hold of the future with honest enthusiasm and a heartfelt anticipation of good things to come.

A New Hope

The women in the original Radical group and almost every other woman in this situation say they need one thing more than anything else—"I just need hope." We all felt a level of hopelessness in the beginning, so if that is your overriding emotion, don't feel alone. It's the ground zero starting point. This book was written to give us all a solid basis for hope. Hope that we can survive. Hope that we won't always feel this horrible, agonizing pain in our hearts, and hope that we can somehow reach a deeper understanding about what life at its best can be.

We want reassurance that God's purpose for our lives is being continually developed, especially through this. By taking hold of God's power within us, by recognizing the wisdom of the ages and by taking courage from the examples of women who have survived and blossomed during this ordeal, we can all have hope.

But first we have to survive. First we have to make the decision that this detour will not destroy us, but instead will make us stronger and more loving and more joyful than we have ever been. This book's purpose is *not* to help you survive until you get into another relationship. It will help you realize that you have the power regardless of any outward circumstances to choose joy and to choose fun and to choose goodness, peace, contentment and an excited anticipation about life. Even if you're living paycheck to paycheck. Even if your husband marries a beautiful skinny woman half your age. Even if your children go spend Christmas with him and his girlfriend at the home you helped build and decorate. Even if you are single the rest of your life.

So, first of all, set your sights on a new hope. This Radical Recovery book can help you get through the next few minutes and hours and days and months, and, of course, all the nights. The process is not easy. It doesn't happen overnight. It takes time to come to grips with the devastation of lost dreams. Divorce is a death that must be mourned before we can move on. It's a grief-filled road that simply has to be traveled.

This book is not magic, but it will help you on your journey. It's not just a self-help book. It utilizes a Radical approach to achieve Radical results. It applies Radical principles to discover Radical joy. It takes a life-shaking, life-changing experience and finds ways to use that experience to teach us to fully appreciate and share this feast of life. But to get to where you want to be, you can't avoid the hard—but liberating—work of recovery and renewal.

Right now you may be thinking that nothing worth the terrible losses will ever come from this. But let me assure you, life can be good again. Life can be full of wonder and beautiful amazement and honest-to-goodness laughter again. It doesn't seem possible from where you are right now, I know. But it has happened in my life and in the lives of other Radical Women. One of the first women in our Radical group said, "I would not wish this on anyone, but I wouldn't give it up even with all of the anguish and pain, because it has brought me a new relationship with God and with people that I would never have had. It has changed my life in a way that's worth everything." Now that's a glimmer of hope!

Our goal is to use the unwanted experience of midlife divorce to develop a fresh understanding of the magnificence and preciousness of life. Many women, unfortunately, stay angry and full of hatred and despair until the bitter end—literally. But what good is that? Life isn't fair. It never has been. It never will be. We can either moan and groan endlessly about that, or we can lift our heads up, put our shoulders back and say, "I don't have long on this earth, and I am going to make the best of every single day no matter what!"

Let him and his girlfriend live their shallow, little pitiful life. Let them live the weak, embarrassing life they've chosen. *You* deserve something better. You know what real love and life are about, and you can demonstrate to those around you that you won't let the smallness of someone else's actions destroy your goodness and grace. You can either die a slow lifelong death of ugliness and remorse, or you can live every minute of life as a glorious gift to enjoy and appreciate and share.

Another thing that helped all of us was the simple act of sharing our stories. If you are reading this book and have not shared your situation with anyone, you should. I did not tell anyone for more than six months, and it would have been easier if I had. Talk to a trusted friend or family member. Talk to someone at your church. Find a counselor.

In the beginning, my husband and I met with a counselor who was seeing us both individually and as a couple. He was also seeing other people connected to the situation. Although he gave me solid, helpful advice and talked me through some very tough days, I decided he had too many irons in the fire, and I got my own counselor. She is a Christian counselor who never quoted one Bible verse, but has definite Christian values. She was down-to-earth and straightforward. She let me cry. She made me laugh. She was invaluable in guiding me toward the hard decisions I needed to make.

Using plain English, she helped me see the situation as it was, instead of how I wanted it to be, and she gave me confidence to make godly decisions based on that reality. She was an incredible resource during all of this and turned out to be a good friend. Also, if your marriage cannot be mended, find a good attorney who is fair, but who will stand up for you and negotiate strongly on your behalf. My attorney was compassionate, bright and professional. Her ultimate goal was to get me the best settlement possible. Find an advocate like that. Remember, it is your life. You have to make the final choices about the professionals you hire, and about what they do.

And, while you're at it, find a good dependable plumber.

A WORD OF CAUTION

Several years of Radical meetings and individual conversations resulted in this book. Not everyone approached things from a spiritual perspective as I did. There are women who don't believe in God, or who don't think God really works in our lives. Some don't have any opinion at all. Some people told me, "Don't talk about God—you'll turn people off." To speak of Jesus might seem to alienate all non-Christians. I don't mean to do that, but Christ is my hope. Whether you are a Christian or not, the principles of Christianity can bring you abundance and peace.

All I know is that I could not have made it through this ordeal without God. I was struggling to get through every hour of every day and every night. Believing that there is a God who created me and formed me and redeemed me and who knows my name and the number of hairs on my head and sees my every tear, brings me a confidence I would have no other way. It gives meaning to the suffering. It gives hope that the sadness may be used for good in the long run.

Some of you reading this may feel you can handle your situation on your own. I couldn't. I was so sad and so angry and so hurt that I wasn't doing well with anything. Some days I could have strangled both my husband and his girlfriend. In my mind it would have been justified, but I don't believe that's the message God wants me to tell. The message he wants me to broadcast is that love is the best way, and that rage and revenge and ugliness will not bring the joy I desire into anyone's life, especially my own. Those reaping and sowing laws are true no matter what your religious background.

We rarely talked about God in our actual Radical meetings. We talked more about what to do with the Christmas stockings and the family pictures, what to do about health insurance, and how to survive sharing our children with his girlfriend. This book turned out to be a handbook of survival strategies from all the Radical Women, and also a record of my own spiritual journey to joy.

So if you are reading this Radical guide, use what parts of it you can. Skip over the rest. The concepts in this book have helped others and me, and I hope they will help you. God doesn't solve our problems. He gives us the power to do that ourselves. God doesn't make everyone do just what we want them to, but he does give us guideposts of behavior that will bring joy and contentment into our lives no matter what anyone else is doing. Some days during this mess, I simply could not conjure up that assurance on my own. Some days I couldn't stop crying long enough to formulate any positive thought at all. Some days, my belief in God was absolutely the only thing that I could hold on to that gave me any peace. To me it was a lifeline to hope—and at a time when I was barely holding on.

Another benefit of believing in God is that he expects us to take control in our lives. We become proactive and stop being victims. I believe God expects us to be his ambassadors in this world. He doesn't want us to be weak, sniveling, wimpy people. He expects us, as his beloved children, to be bold and strong enough to tell his story and be his good cheer in a world that is often unfair and hurtful and selfish and mean. What this situation is helping me learn is that God wants to use us and bless us and give us an abundance we can't even imagine.

If that's too religious, or too much God for you, maybe you should look for help in a different book. But for those of you who are willing to search for the big picture in all of this, and are willing to be strong enough to get the victory against all odds, and to show your children and your friends and your world that you will rise above this with unbelievable peace, and undeniable joy, and a rich, full love, then read on. Get ready for the battle, and expect an amazing triumph in your life.

Okay, let's get started!

Chapter One

FIRST, SURVIVE

First, survive.

*Then try to get
through this ordeal
without killing anybody…
or allowing anybody
to destroy you.*

Those long agonized seconds in the mornings when I first came back to consciousness after the restless nights were the seconds I hated most. I dreaded those gut-wrenching moments when I first realized—again—that my husband was having an affair, that he would not end it, and that the life I had known for 33 years was crumbling all around me.

I would cover my head in despair and think, "Oh God! It's true." I would sometimes think, "I can't do this again today. I can't face this again today. Please don't make me get up again today. Please let me lose consciousness until it doesn't hurt so much, and then I'll get up!" But somehow, after dealing with those first awful moments of realization, I would try to find the strength and courage to get my feet on the floor. Some days I did better than others.

Our three oldest children were on their own—either married or in medical school or working and making their own way—but our youngest son was in middle school and high school during all of this. The days he was at home, it was easier to make myself get up. He gave me a real-life reason to get out of bed. I was trying hard to show all of my children that God could be trusted, even though at the moment he didn't seem to be working out my life to my satisfaction. I wanted them to realize that because we have a God who loves us and works in our lives for his glory and our good, we can meet every day with confidence and joy.

I will admit, however, I was feeling neither confidence nor joy most of the time. I was feeling mostly agony and despair. I guess I was sort of faking it, on the surface, at least. Deep in my heart I believed God was working on my behalf, but I hated how this was going. I hated the fact that he hadn't miraculously stepped in and fixed things—like I wanted them to be fixed, anyway.

Occasionally, in those dark hours I would say, "God, I've tried to be your person. I've tried to do what you want. Is this what I get—agony and despair and this incredible ache in my heart—this hurting in every fiber of my being? Is this what I get for following you? Why aren't you fixing this so we can be an example to others, so we can tell our story of victory to other couples facing this? You tell us in the Psalms that if we trust you, you will give us 'the desires of our heart.' It's my heart's desire to have a strong, bright shining marriage. Where are you? Why aren't you doing anything to help?"

But day after day, especially in the mornings, I would face the reality that God was allowing me to struggle with this situation, that my husband was continuing his affair, and that our marriage was ending.

The Survival Six
1. GET UP

Each morning I had to mentally and physically will myself out of bed. You will have to do that, too. Will yourself out of that temporary, restive cocoon. After you're up, I'll guarantee that the rest of the minutes of the day will present challenges and heartaches of their own, but at least you will have that small, but significant, victory of getting in the ring for another round. You will have reassured yourself, and those around you, that you have the power and the courage not only to face this, but also to be stronger and more beautiful because of it in the end. Step one is getting out of bed every day. Copy the list on the next page and post it to remind you of the Survival Six. All of them are discussed in additional detail below.

In the early days of her separation and divorce, one of the women in our first Radical group had a friend who came over and helped get her out of bed and helped get her children off to school. At one of our meetings, she said simply, "I just couldn't do it on my own. I felt paralyzed, even though I knew I needed to be strong for my children. I felt like I was actually physically and emotionally falling apart." Another member of the group said, "The day I realized he was really going to leave our family and marry his girlfriend, I just kept telling myself over and over again, 'Breathe! Breathe! Breathe!'"

During the first weeks of this ordeal, life literally gets down to the basics. It's a physical, emotional, spiritual battle for survival. On many occasions, friends and members of my family would call or e-mail or send cards or come for a few days of support. Whatever it takes, call on the people you need.

Don't be embarrassed to ask for help. But begin by getting your body upright and out of bed every day.

It helped me to think about this verse in Romans, "Get out of bed and get dressed! Don't loiter and linger waiting until the very last minute. Dress yourselves in Christ and be up and about." So, whatever it takes, make the decision to survive, and get up! Keep a scripture or an inspirational thought or a short prayer by your bed and read it the very first thing in the morning. Believe that God will help you get your feet on the floor, and that he will give you power for the rest of the day as well. That belief will become reality.

THE RADICAL WOMAN'S
Survival Six:

1. Get Up

2. Take a Shower

3. Fix Your Face

4. Get Dressed

5. Eat Something Healthy

6. Get Moving

The Survival Six

2. TAKE A SHOWER

Once you're out of bed, go directly into the bathroom, turn on the water and step into the shower. Don't even think about it ... just do it! Baths are nice for the evening hours, but for the morning, getting into the shower is a positive step toward meeting the battles of the day. There is therapeutic value in water. Let the warm water rush over you. It can rejuvenate you and get you ready to face whatever you will be called on to face, however woefully unprepared you seem at the moment. Even if you haven't slept very well, a shower will give you a renewed sense of energy and confidence. Try a cool rinse at the end for a little extra jolt.

When you first step in the shower, stand there a minute or so and feel the water flow over your head and your body. Imagine the water washing away any hateful, hurtful, harmful feelings you might have. Visualize all of your negative thoughts and feelings going down the drain. Get physically clean and get emotionally and mentally clean and prepared at the same time. You're going to have to face the day whether you're ready or not, so you may as well get ready and pamper yourself in the process.

Washing rituals have been a part of religious practices for thousands of years. Jewish and Christian traditions both have references to washing ourselves not only clean of physical impurities, but spiritual ones too. The prophet Jeremiah advised the Israelites, "O Jerusalem, wash the evil from your heart and be saved. How long will you harbor wicked thoughts?" Every one of us in the Radical group agreed we had harbored more than a few wicked thoughts during all of this!

In Psalms 51, David says to God, "Cleanse me with hyssop, and I will be clean; wash me, and I will be whiter than snow. Let me hear joy and gladness; Create in me a pure heart, O God, and renew a steadfast spirit within me." All of us, in this situation need a new heart and a new spirit within us.

Our bodies feel betrayed—our hearts feel heavy—our thoughts are bogged down with sadness and anger. Let's take a lesson from major religious traditions and understand the importance of being clean in our hearts and in our spirits. Use the simple act of taking a shower as a catalyst for renewing your mind and your heart as you start each new day.

To make the most of this daily experience, splurge on a bar of fragrant hand-milled soap. Bath shops have soaps to fit every individual preference. There are soaps scented for an invigorating uplift, or for a relaxing calm, or for an overall sense of well-being. There are bars of every shape and size scented for your preferences—woodsy, oriental, musky, flowery, herbal and almost everything else imaginable. Totally pamper yourself. Buy whatever soap you want from your favorite bath shop. That simple extravagance will be worth every penny. It will help you in some intrinsic way feel more beautiful and fresh. While you're at it, buy a natural loofah or one of those soft mesh sponges and use it to suds up all over. Both the loofah and the sponge stimulate your skin, cleanse away the top layer of dead cells, and give you a sort of tingly feeling. Translate that sensation into an adventurous anticipation of the good things that will happen to you today.

If you can, buy yourself a special towel that is just what you want. I like one that is kind of thin and rough. I like the feel of roughing up my skin a bit as I dry off. It's invigorating. One bath company has what is known as the Japanese body buffing towel. It's used to stimulate the largest sense organ you have, your skin. Some of the Radical Women like big, fluffy bath sheets to wrap themselves up in as they dry off. Through this whole experience, remember that you are still on your two feet, that you still have thousands of things to be thankful for and one of them is this wonderful, pleasure-filled shower.

Start thinking about everything you do today in the same way. Don't take the real pleasures of this day for granted. Completely enjoy the purely sensual sensations of your shower. Focus on your special soap. How does it smell? How does it feel in your hand? Be aware of the temperature and pressure of the water on your skin. Be aware and be thankful. You have your family, your friends, your health, your body, your personality, your imagination, your abilities, your faith, your sense of humor (even though it may be in remission right now), your ability to read, freedom, the privilege of prayer, and your own power to feel things and smell things and totally appreciate the blessings of the moment.

In the movie, *Memoirs of a Geisha*, there is a bit of dialogue that goes like this: an American GI says, "Back home a bath is nothing more than a quick shower on cold tile with lye soap. You make everything a ritual." The Japanese Geisha answers, "That is the art of turning habit into pleasure." Who doesn't remember that spellbinding scene from the movie *Witness*, when the Amish woman creates a breathtaking experience using only a simple washtub of water, soap and a big sudsy sponge. Some cultures have learned to fine-tune their senses to a total appreciation of everyday moments. We should do that, too. Especially now.

For a long time, I have considered a long, leisurely bath or an invigorating shower a very precious luxury. Almost any time I get into a warm bath or stand in the shower with clear water coursing over my head and over my body, I thank God for that remarkable privilege. Think of all of the women all over the world who will never feel that glorious private, personal pleasure. The majority of women on this earth will never have the luxury of a special room where they can shut the door, and maybe lock it, then turn on a rush of fresh, clean, warm water and wash themselves from head to toe. Never take that truly exquisite physical experience for granted, and every time you take a shower, use that time to infuse your life with a renewed attitude of gratitude and peace. Feel the joy of pure, clean water preparing both your outer and your inner self to meet the adventures of the day. Think about the physical pleasures and the spiritual connotations of that simple act.

The Survival Six

3. FIX YOUR FACE

"Fixing" your face means more than one thing. It includes the physiological part—the smiling part—and the physical part—the skin and make-up part. First, let's talk about the physiological part—smiling. I know that most of the time you don't feel like smiling. In fact, what you've probably been doing 24 hours a day every day is trying as hard as you can to keep from crying. It's hard for your face to look good when that is happening.

Thomas Paine said, "I love the man (or woman) who can smile in trouble, who can gather strength from distress, and grow brave by reflection." All the Radical Women were trying to do that, but I'll admit I, for one, wasn't being very successful—especially early on. In the beginning, almost everything makes you cry.

The Radical group discovered something amazing about having a positive attitude. We read in several places that if you can smile when you're feeling down, that act alone can make you feel better, more positive and more optimistic. Most of the time when I first tried it, I felt like a fraud. I am a normally happy, friendly, cheerful person, but during my husband's affair and its aftermath, I didn't feel like putting on a happy face, especially when I was feeling so discouraged and defeated. But slowly, the more I tried the smiling test, the more it seemed to prove true.

> *"We found studies that indicate that when you smile, your brain changes—changes caused merely by the act of turning up the corners of your mouth."*

We found studies that indicate that when you smile, your brain changes—changes caused merely by the act of turning up the corners of your mouth. So, put on a happy face even if you don't feel like it.

Thousands of years ago, the wise man Solomon knew the power of a positive spirit. In Proverbs he says, "A cheerful heart is good medicine, but a crushed spirit dries up the bones." I know for a fact that after the Radical meetings, when we had all really laughed about something, we all felt better.

Here's what will happen if we can't break out of our black moods: our family and friends will get tired of dealing with us. They will give us space for a while, but at some point we all need to get a grip and keep our sadness contained a bit, at least in public. Any time you can find something to smile about, do. Even putting a pencil in your mouth to mimic a smile causes positive things to happen. That seems far-fetched, but apparently it's true.

As with any grieving process, smiling is not the appropriate option all the time. Continually wearing a fake, vacuous smile is unrealistic and counterproductive. People will begin to wonder what mind-altering drug you're on. The point here is to encourage you to make a conscious effort to look for things to be happy about. As time moves forward, finding the joy around you will begin to get easier, and the smile you put on your face will seem more natural.

When a woman is grieving the loss of someone close to her—as all Radical Women are—she needs to cry. Those who don't cry usually don't really get over the loss. Those who try not to ever cry, finally do one day. I used to be afraid that I might start crying and never be able to stop. But you do stop sooner or later. So we're not trying to say, "Don't be sad. Don't cry." We are saying that you have every right to be sad and angry, but eventually you have to figure out how to get over that. I found a ceramic tile when I was in the angry, bitter stage of this process. I still have it by my sink. It says, "Don't carry a grudge, cause while you're carrying a grudge, the other guy's out dancing!" (And probably doing a few other things with his girlfriend, as well!)

So, be mad and sad as long as you need to, then somehow you're going to have to create a strategy to get beyond that. Recognizing and appreciating any simple thing that gives you joy is a step in the right direction.

"Fix your face" means to smile, but it also means making your face look as good as possible. Fixing your face does not mean piling on makeup or using cosmetics that you would not normally use. It does mean have a good complexion system in place for cleaning, freshening and moisturizing your face. I saved up enough money to buy a good product line that I like and that makes my skin feel better. It seems to make me look a bit better, too. It also gives me a definite daily regimen of things to do for my face. During this time, we need the structure of lists and order. It's good to have a defined set of things to do. Haphazard stuff goes by the wayside when you are under emotional stress like this. Early on, there were days I actually forgot to brush my teeth, and occasionally I'd wonder in the grocery line or at the drycleaners, "Did I comb my hair?" So for now any system that has a certain regimen to follow is best.

Fixing your face might mean using cold cucumbers or chilled cotton pads soaked in witch hazel to keep your eyes looking fresh and bright. One of the Radical Women told a story about an emotional day that had included significant tears and trauma. (So what's new?) That evening she was supposed to preside as chairman of a meeting at the high school. Her eyes looked red and terrible, so she sent her 17-year-old son to the drug store to get some of those pads for hemorrhoid sufferers. "They work wonders if you chill them and put them on your eyes for 15 minutes or so," she said. Her son went to the drug store, bought the assigned product, and told his Mom he made sure the clerk knew that the pads were not for him. Aren't our children wonderful? There are also products designed specifically to help if you have puffy, red eyes. Keep some pads like one of these on hand for emergencies.

Another simple, obvious piece of advice is to invest in plenty of tissues. Keep them close by—in your car, at your desk, by your bed, in the kitchen, in the laundry room, in your purse, in your bike bag—you get the picture.

It's hard to look good when you are sad and angry so much of the time. Part of the strategy in looking presentable is to be prepared for the things that make you emotional. In the beginning of this ordeal, almost everything has the potential to make you either unbearably sad or unbelievably angry. Neither one is good for our faces.

I could hardly listen to music through all of this. For people of all ages, music is a connection to the past and a direct link to our deepest feelings and most intimate memories and experiences.

My husband and I had been married for more than three decades, and we both loved music. Every era of music brought back memories that made me cry. I couldn't listen to 60s, 70s, 80s, or 90s music. I couldn't listen to our favorite groups. I couldn't listen to rock, bluegrass, show tunes, John Denver, The Beach Boys, The Eagles, Janis Joplin, songs like "Bridge Over

Troubled Waters," songs from *The Graduate* or *Fame* or *Hair*. I couldn't listen to Classical Gas or Layla or Joe Cocker or Leon Russell or The Band without a big lump in my throat.

I remember one time hearing a song that upset me terribly and hitting the steering wheel, crying and furious that I couldn't even listen to music I loved. I was not the one having the affair, but I was the one suffering every single day because of it! The only things I could listen to on the radio were jazz, black gospel and Christian stations—or if I were desperate, Talk Radio. My youngest son looked at my selection of CDs in the car one day and told me bluntly that I needed to get some new songs. He has since made me some personalized CDs of my own that I love. I have also managed to find a few artists and groups that I am creating new connections with, but I still can't enjoy all that great music from the past like I used to. Maybe a little further down the line I can.

Even though music and almost everything else made me sad at the beginning, I only had a couple of days when I really felt emotionally out of control—with sadness, that is. I was out of control with rage on more than a few occasions, but that's for another chapter.

One time when I couldn't control my sadness was when the appraiser came to appraise the house that my husband and I had designed and built together. In our divorce agreement, I was to get the house, but I knew I would have to sell it. After the divorce, there would be no way I could keep it. The house had become a huge basketful of memories. Fifteen years of fantastic, nourishing family memories, and lately ugly, agonizing memories. I knew we needed to get out of our house, but the day the appraiser came, the house looked great, and I mourned in my heart every single thing I cherished about that house and most of the things that had happened there.

I thought of all the family milestones and celebrations in the rooms of that house. Graduations. Proms. Christmas parties. Reunions. Weddings. New grandchildren. Business projects. Good news. Kids playing the piano. Neighborhood friendships. School functions. Soccer games. Special Dinners.

> *"...I ended up on the floor of the closet, moaning, sobbing, holding myself, rocking back and forth like the women you see on television in those news stories about some horrible disaster in a faraway country."*

Birthdays. Anniversaries. In total, I thought of all those family memories that happen throughout the years that make your house your own personal haven of belonging and joy.

I thought about the features of the house I loved, and would miss. We had carefully planned the house, and because of my background in art, I enjoyed choosing the colors and the carpets and the wallpaper and even the hardware and the light fixtures. I cherished the opportunity to design and compose our family living space. I loved the old stained glass windows I found for the built-in cupboards in the dining room. The bricks from our old house that we put in the hearth at this house. The windows I designed for the front entry. My art room that looked out on big trees. The back deck. The creek in the back that was a kid's paradise. The table outside where our oldest son had proposed to his amazing wife. The kitchen where our hearts met most often—our bedroom where we shared so many of the intimacies of life—the laundry room where laundry piled up more than it should have. All the colors and spaces I loved.

Suddenly, I was sick with loss about leaving the house and all of its memories, but I was devastated most of all about losing my dreams for our family and knowing that our family would never be the same.

When the appraiser came, I remember going into the closet in my daughter's room to try to pull myself together. Every time I came out of the closet I started crying again. One of our sons, who happened to be home from college, had to take the appraiser around the house. Finally, I ended up on the floor of the closet, moaning, sobbing, holding myself, rocking back and forth like the women you see on television in those news stories about some horrible disaster in a faraway country.

I was so full of pain I couldn't quite get control of myself. Later after the appraiser had gone, our middle son came into the closet, sat down beside me, put his arm around me and said, "Mom, are you going to trust God or not?"

My son's question hit me like a shocking slap in the face, even though he said it with absolutely no reproach in his voice. For all of those years, I had tried to teach our children that God could be trusted—that we had to commit to him, obey him the best we could and trust him to work out the rest. And here I was on the floor of the closet, barely able to hold myself together. My spirit wanted to trust God. But my physical self was so sad about the end of our marriage that I had a hard time believing that God could bring something good out of this. I wanted to trust him. I was trying to. But at that moment on that day, I was overwhelmed with grief over the loss of everything I dreamed my life would be.

I realized that at 53, after 33 years of marriage, my husband wanted another woman; we were getting a divorce; and all of my thoughts about growing old together and doing all kinds of fun things together were gone.

No amount of skin care or fixing up could have made my face look any better that day, and thankfully I didn't have to go anywhere that night. Putting a smile on my face wouldn't have worked either. I couldn't have, even if I had thought about trying. I was absolutely too miserable. Some days you just have to struggle through the best you can—and if you end the day still in one piece, it's a victory.

The Survival Six

4. GET DRESSED

Now, a few words about dressing. My husband began this affair when we had been married 30 years. I was 50 years old. Half a century old. Even though I was 50, I felt confident. I was in good shape. I worked out. I walked with my head high and felt good about myself. I stayed up with the times. My background is in graphic design, and I have studied art all through my academic and professional career. My style of dress—my style of everything—

is well, sort of artistic, or maybe, funky. Eclectic is the word, I think. I like simple, clean lines, with no fluff, but with a bit of surprise.

After I found out about my husband's continuing affair, I suddenly didn't feel like being funky or fun. I could hardly wear jewelry. In the mornings when I was trying to figure out what to wear, I felt the same way I feel when I'm getting dressed to attend a funeral. No bright colors. No artsy jewelry. No fun. No funk. No fashion statements or surprises. In other words, drab. That's how I felt. That's what I saw when I looked in the mirror. Not funky. Frumpy.

My husband's affair suddenly made me feel old and ugly and fat. His skinny, long-legged blond girlfriend made me feel unsure of myself, and somehow embarrassed about how I looked. I thought, "Maybe I look terrible. Maybe I'm not as much fun as I thought I was. Everyone in the world knows he left me for another woman. Maybe everyone thinks I'm a terrible witch at home or no good in bed or a stick in the mud. Maybe, I'm just not good-looking enough."

I knew, or at least hoped in my heart, that this kind of thinking was ridiculous, but the Radical Women found that we all felt some variation of that. It's as if you suddenly aren't cool enough or fun enough or good enough to deserve your husband's faithfulness, even after all those years.

We all somehow wished we were thinner or prettier or younger. Some of the husbands' girlfriends were young enough to be their daughters. Or they were exotic women named Alexandra. Or size four administrative assistants who were misunderstood by their husbands—or sad, unfulfilled nurses. How can any wife, busy with life, possibly compete with someone whose only desire is to please and entice your husband—and who sometimes has more in common with your daughter than with you?

I'll admit that during this time I wanted to look good. I didn't just want to look nice, but I wanted to look classy, sexy and appealing as well. What I really wanted was for my husband to want me again. But when I stood in front of the closet trying to figure out what to put on for the day, just like nothing sounded good to eat, nothing sounded good to wear.

At one of our Radical meetings we talked about how one could usually spot divorced women, especially ones who had been divorced several years. They start dressing too tight and too young, and trying too hard to be hip. There is a name for this in Internet speak. It's called "teenile," and the definition is someone who is way too old for what they are wearing. Divorcees often start going to bars, nightspots or trendy restaurants, sitting together, talking too loudly and acting too much like they are having fun. You've seen them, I'm sure. You can usually catch them looking out of the corner of their eye to see if anyone is noticing. There's a subtle sense of desperation.

I hate to see that. It's sad and makes my heart ache because I know how easy it is to try to be someone you're not, or to try to prove you're still okay, when you are really only trying to muster up some tiny bit of self esteem in the face of this devastation.

While my husband and I were separated, I was a member of my local Chamber of Commerce. I had volunteered to help at an evening social gathering of the group. I was working the front desk signing people in and giving them their name tags and materials. As it happened, the other two volunteers were two divorced women about my age who had been divorced a fairly long time. They acted ridiculous. They, of course, acted like they were just having a ball—laughing very loudly, being too flirtatious, wearing clingy shirts that were too blatantly revealing. Every guy who came in alone became the target of their running commentary about "his body, his great hair, his beautiful eyes," and such. They were acting like teenagers—and not even mature teenagers. I was embarrassed, and I couldn't wait for my time slot to be over.

So, when you get up in the morning, make an effort to really get dressed. Don't just throw something on without any thought. Update your wardrobe a little if you can afford to. Get rid of stuff you never wear. Start dressing exactly how you want. Don't go off the deep end and totally change your style, or try to be someone you're not by the clothes you wear, but start making the choices about how you want to look.

A *Wall Street Journal* article entitled, "Office Fashion Tip: Looking Grown Up Whatever Your Age," quotes Evie Gorenstein, who runs a shopping service for a designer discount store, "If you're 50 and trying to look 30, you're going to look older than 50." As for dressing age-appropriately, she believes "what counts most is being fit and having a developed sense of style—and that often doesn't happen until you're at least 40 and more experienced." So, figure out your style. Refine it. Be proud of it!

When you're married, sometimes you find yourself dressing to please your husband as much as dressing to please yourself. One year for Christmas my then husband went completely overboard and bought me several outfits. These outfits were all very tailored wool pants and jackets and very tailored skirts with very traditional sweaters and blouses. I appreciated every single thing, but they just were not me—at all. I couldn't believe he had lived with me for all of those years and had no idea what I liked, or that he didn't care what I liked. I don't know which option distressed me more. Since our divorce, I've passed along every one of those outfits. I was happy to get them out of my closet. Not only were they not my style, none of them were very comfortable to wear!

Now is the time to discover what *you* like—what style is really you. You aren't dressing to please anyone else right now, so please yourself. If you can, go get a dynamite new outfit. Take a fun, bold, stylish friend shopping with you and get something just because you like it. Think about what textures and colors and styles you are drawn to. Be adventurous. I know money may be tight right now. If so, try a really cool resale shop. Don't go completely berserk, and don't spend more than you should, but think just about yourself for once and only buy things that make *you* feel great. Put your shoulders back and walk with renewed optimism and hope. You are a good, worthy, fun person. Dress like it. Act like it.

When you are deciding what to wear in the mornings, look at yourself without anything on in front of a full-length mirror. Stand straight and proud. Smile. Really smile so your eyes crinkle up! There are always details about ourselves that we would like to improve, but rejoice in exactly who you are this moment. Make a conscious decision to live like you want to today. If you need to lose weight or get in better shape, or get new glasses, or get your hair cut, you can. It's never too late. But remember that you are a beautiful person just as you are right this minute. Your beauty shines through in how you act, in how you care for other people, in how you approach life. God has made you exactly who you are, so be proud of that, and let him use you to accomplish his purposes whatever they might be today.

> *"Walking, talking, smiling with confidence is actually very seductive— it gets us and those we meet in the mood for fun and enjoyment."*

Most research says that confidence is one of the most appealing things about any woman. Walking, talking, smiling with confidence is actually very seductive—it gets us and those we meet in the mood for fun and enjoyment. We aren't overly stressed about the impression we're making. We are instead "out of ourselves" enjoying the moment, learning something new or getting to know someone better. What most people want is for the person they are talking with to be interested in them, to appreciate them, to care about them. You have every reason to be confident. You are a child of God. He made you uniquely you, and he wants to use who you are to bless other people. So go ahead. Get dressed. Say with the Psalmist, "This is the day the Lord has made, I will rejoice and be glad in it" and smile and walk and live like you mean it.

The Survival Six

5. EAT SOMETHING HEALTHY

It may be that *nothing* sounds good to eat during this upheaval. Or it may be that *everything* sounds good to eat—and eating is your comfort. Either way, you must make sure you eat something and that what you do eat will give you the energy and strength you need.

Almost all of the Radical women lost weight, especially in the beginning. However, one of our group temporarily turned to food for comfort and escape when her executive husband decided he wanted to leave her and live with a redhead who was near the age of one of their daughters.

Our funny, funky friend, who overdid the comfort food for a while, grew up in a family where normal forms of caring and comfort were almost non-existent. She said, "If it hadn't been for the consolation food brought, there would have been no consolation at all." She got control of that particular problem and is now at a good weight again and has new adventure, fun and "blessings overflowing everywhere" in her life. She is one of my favorite people and she has a great sense of humor.

Personally, for the only time in my life except the first few months I was pregnant with my second and fourth children, food was of no interest to me. I was so overcome with my life situation that I had no desire to eat, or I would simply forget to eat. I felt sick to my stomach almost every day. I thought, too, that I would look better if I lost some weight. You probably have some of those feelings, as well.

Even though most of the Radical Women were physically fit and a normal weight, for some reason all of the girlfriends and mistresses seemed to be especially thin. Maybe that's just how we imagined them, because I for one always wanted to be thinner. It's okay to lose some weight during this time. Almost all of us could stand to shed a few pounds, but don't let it get out of control. Try to make the things you eat nutritious.

Although some nights it's okay to give in to the temptation, don't eat ice cream with hot fudge sauce and pecans every night. I found myself eating buttered popcorn often. For some reason, that tasted okay to me. Many nights I ate a little chunk of cheese, some hard bread or crackers and a glass of wine. It was quick, easy and it made me relax a little. Be sure you don't overdo the wine—or whatever you might be drinking. That is one habit that would be easy to slip into during this crisis.

Occasionally, the counselor my husband and I were seeing at first would schedule my individual session over the lunch hour and either bring, or have me pick up, a sandwich on the way. The plan was that we would eat and talk, and he would, I guess, do his part to make sure I didn't waste away. Usually he would eat, and I would pick around on whatever was in front of me. Almost invariably I cried during those sessions, and it was hard to cry and eat at the same time. I lost those ten pounds that I had tried to lose for decades. In fact, I lost 20 pounds. That is one good thing that came out of those awful years.

When our youngest was home, I did a little better with the food thing because I cooked for him. I never stopped cooking, really; I just didn't eat much. One of my friends who has been a grief counselor for many years, said to me that when people are grieving, they lose touch with their senses. The sense of smell is not as keen as usual, and taste, especially, is off-balance. I know for me, almost anything I ate tasted bland. Nothing tasted really good. Things that had always smelled delicious suddenly didn't, so I just didn't eat and I didn't miss it.

On the other end of the spectrum, when I did cook, I couldn't get out of the habit of cooking for a family. I would end up with enough to feed an army for just two of us. I find myself making way too much of everything, even now. I still miss sitting down together with the family for a meal. That was always important to me growing up and was especially so after we had a family of our own with everyone going ten different directions.

During this upheaval, I worried that my son still at home felt cheated. It was often just the two of us eating together in the kitchen. Like most kids in high school, he was so active and involved in high school life that he didn't complain. We also had, and still have, lots of family gatherings at our house or at his siblings' houses, so maybe that has helped, too. I personally thought our dinners were a blessing and a privilege, and were for me a very precious time to just eat a good meal and talk about our respective days. I also loved the days he brought a friend or two home to dinner with him.

Some advice from all of us is to try eating six small meals a day instead of three bigger ones. It's been proven that eating small meals throughout the day is better for all of your physiological systems anyway. Blood sugar is more regulated; it is easier on the digestive system, and has other benefits as well.

Try eating a piece of fruit during the day or a hard boiled egg or some almonds or dried apricots or a fresh tomato with cottage cheese, or some carrot sticks, radishes, a bowl of cereal or chicken noodle soup. Simple stuff. Things you don't have to work to prepare. Concentrate on whole grains. Get plenty of calcium. Think healthy. Pretend you are at an exclusive spa resort, and you are there to eat healthy, nutritious food that will help you lose weight and feel better. If you are still cooking for children, occasionally think of wonderful, warm, filling, comfort food like homemade macaroni and cheese or chicken and noodles. They will taste good to you, too. Have your kids help in the kitchen if you can. It's a relaxed, comfortable time to talk about their day and yours. Keep the conversation light-hearted and fun if you possibly can.

> *"Have your kids help in the kitchen if you can. It's a relaxed, comfortable time to talk about their day and yours."*

Sometimes during this crisis, cherished, wonderful friends called me on the phone to see if I would go get a bite to eat. I always, always appreciated that more than they knew. Sometimes some of the Radical Women got together in one of our homes and had a simple dinner together. Eating alone after years of having a husband and family takes a lot of getting used to. I would usually try to read if I were by myself, or very rarely I would watch television, although that was something I didn't encourage when our family was growing up, and it sort of felt like a cop-out doing it now. I felt like my children would somehow be disappointed if they knew!

I have a series of great old antique books published in 1894 called *Great Men and Famous Women*. These books have fantastic illustrations with thin tissue cover sheets, and the books have little histories of great people from the beginning of recorded history until 1894. Each vignette is about four or five pages long. The books are big—nine inches by 12 inches—and beautifully leather-bound. I began to read about the life of one great person as I ate lunch or dinner every day and learned so much in the process. I felt like I was getting sustenance for my mind as well as my body. If you are alone, get a big book at the bookstore about some topic you are interested in (check the sale table) and read part of it each day as you eat. It will improve your mind and give you something concrete to think about besides what your ex-husband and his girlfriend are doing!

There is a little neighborhood restaurant near my house that has about 20 tables and is located two doors down from one of my favorite bookstores. I love the classical music played in this place, and the ambience is very comfortable—almost European. I would sometimes get a magazine at the bookstore and then go get something to eat when the restaurant first opened in the evening about 5 p.m. The first time I went there by myself, I told my waitress that my husband was out of town, which he was, and my kids gone for the evening, which they were, so I decided to treat myself.

Afterwards, I didn't feel I always had to explain myself. I began to think of this as a personal luxury. No one else had to know that I was there because I had no one at home and could not stand eating another dinner by myself in my quiet, empty house. Before long, I got to know the owners and the chef, and I could sit at one of the tall tables by the dessert case. I wasn't out there like a sore thumb among all of the couples and families.

Anyway, it was usually slow at that time of the evening, and I would eat at least *something* since I'd paid for it, and I could take the rest home. They had desserts like Chocolate Bourbon Pecan Pie and a wonderful crunchy coconut crusted pie and any number of other fantastic concoctions.

Even though this trauma in your life was not planned to improve your eating habits, you can use it to do just that. During this time, reevaluate how you eat. Start from scratch. You can make everything you eat something that is good for you. You can rest assured that doing without food for short periods of time won't hurt you and has even been proven to improve your health. Many religions practice fasting in some form or another. Scientific studies have shown that mice that regularly skip meals live longer, so use this time to get rid of habits like eating chips or candy or drinking soft drinks all day.

Make the calories you do eat count for something. You will lose some weight, and that's great, but think of this as a life improvement seminar and not the product of a major midlife meltdown. Just be sure to be vigilant, and don't let the eating situation—either eating too much or too little—turn into a serious problem for you.

The Survival Six
6. Get Moving

I know it's tempting to get back in bed or to just sit around all day. I didn't want to do that, but it seemed to take a huge amount of energy, not only to get from here to there, but also to get from anywhere to anywhere else. In fact, it took unbelievable energy to get out of bed or off the couch.

All of the original Radical Women are vibrant, bright, fun, energetic women who are not accustomed to just sitting around. But for me, the grief of my situation seemed to make my arms and legs feel like weights, and it was the same for everyone else in the group. It seemed to take all the mental and physical energy we had just to go to the grocery store. If you have children at home, it's easier. You have to get up. You have to get them to school. You have to see to their needs. But once they are on the bus or out the door, activity seems to suddenly get harder all over again.

If your children are in college or married or living on their own, finding purpose in the day is oftentimes very hard to do. The ones of you who have full-time jobs have a reason to get moving—you'll most likely get fired if you don't! Of course, the strain of working during this crisis can be a great stress-producing issue in and of itself. But working can provide structure for the day, people to be around, and something to think about other than your own problems—if you can concentrate, that is.

But those of us who are looking for work or are not even that far along in the process don't have a job to go to. During all of this, I was running my business from home, and it was so, so hard to motivate myself to work on some days. All I really wanted to do was get back in bed and try to escape by pulling the covers over my head.

All of us felt that making ourselves get moving was a big step in the right direction. Even though we often didn't feel like doing anything specific, if we made ourselves do *anything*, it was a help. When I was in the separation, pre-divorce stage, I was trying mostly to figure out what was going on. I was trying to figure out if I could live with a man who had a girlfriend who was "the light of his life" and his "best friend." I hated facing the days by myself in our empty house obsessed with what I could do to make him come to his senses or trying desperately to get some quality work done for my clients. Most days I literally made myself get up, take a shower, fix my face, get dressed and then go somewhere—anywhere.

At first, after our son went to school, the place I usually chose to go was a favorite coffee shop about 10 blocks from our house. I would take my *Wall Street Journal*, my neighborhood paper and my daily planner, and I would head out the door for coffee and usually a lemon cherry scone. In the beginning, nothing tasted good, and I would always get the same thing whether I ate it or not. Slowly I expanded my horizons and would sometimes try a blueberry muffin or a pecan sticky bun and whatever special dark roast coffee they were featuring that day. Believe it or not, those small, insignificant choices were very hard to make in the beginning. Even though I probably looked like death warmed over because my nights were usually awful, people were amazingly friendly and cheerful. That helped. And, you're less likely to lose control and start sobbing in the middle of a bustling, morning coffee place.

You'll be surprised how many people stop by the local coffee shop for their morning fix. One of the side benefits was that I started making some new friends there. I would usually start out by sitting at a table by myself, and I had an excuse for that with the papers to get through and my day to plan. At least I was up and walking around and making myself interact with the inhabitants of the land of the living. If the weather was nice, I would sit outside and feel the morning sun on my face, which gave me another little breath of optimism. Gradually, I felt comfortable enough with some of the regulars to tell them my story. People are incredibly empathetic if you give them the chance. Most people want to be helpful, especially people who tend to socialize at the corner coffee shop.

After awhile, I decided I would get a membership at the local health club, so that changed my morning get moving routine. Since our youngest son was in cross country in the fall, swimming in the winter and track in the spring, I decided to get myself in shape as well.

I was trying to look as good as possible, too, because I thought, "Maybe it's her body that is making him do this; maybe if I look better, he'll want me again," or something ridiculous like that. "Maybe, he will come to his senses if I look a little more fit."

I also thought, "If our 17-year-old son can go work out at 5 in the morning, I certainly can too." The trouble was, my body didn't always think, "I certainly can, too." But those days that I made myself go, which was almost every morning, I would definitely feel better after I worked out. I felt tired, but stronger. I was sweaty and out of breath, but more energized. Working my muscles was good for my outlook, even though at first I occasionally cried quietly as I did my paces on the treadmill.

I became one of the regulars there, too, and my world expanded a bit more as my body became more toned. However, I remember the first Valentine's Day after our separation. I was scheduled to meet with the trainer at the gym to check my progress and make sure I was still doing the exercises right. On the way to the gym I saw delivery cars filled with Valentine flowers and balloons, and flowers were on the front desk when I walked in. By the time my trainer got there, I said with a shaky voice, "I'm sorry, I just can't do this today." I cried my way home and thought, "I hate it that I'm not anyone's Valentine," and wondered what my husband got his girlfriend on that special day.

My husband's counselor told him that health clubs and coffee shops are the new pickup places for singles. That was the farthest thing from my mind when my husband asked one day if that's why I was going to those places. I was simply afraid that if I didn't make the effort to get back to life, I would quietly rot away, and I was secretly worried no one would even notice. I didn't tell him that.

On some days during nice weather, I would get on my bike, usually around lunchtime, and ride for at least 10 or 15 miles. Sometimes I would do 22. I would ride as hard as I could for as long as I could, and amazingly, that helped my outlook too. And I was getting stronger. During those days I was in the middle of the very worst parts of my husband's deceptions, so I either cried or begged God to fix things or yelled in the wind as I pedaled. As I rode, I often thought about things I wanted to say to both my husband and his soulmate girlfriend. It was probably good nobody heard me. Anyway, my body began looking sleeker, and the rides made me feel better, too. I told Ariel at the bike shop that I was biking through my divorce, and that biking had helped save my life and my sanity. In some ways, it was true.

"As I rode, I often thought about things I wanted to say to both my husband and his soulmate girlfriend. It was probably good nobody heard me."

So, even if you don't feel like it ... especially if you don't feel like it, get out there and *Get Moving!* Bike, workout, walk with friends or just go down to the local coffee shop—anything. Just get your body out the door and get moving somewhere!

And now, two more lists to help keep you on track during this overwhelming time. "The Body Basics" are must-do items to take care of your health. "Beyond the Basics" includes nice things to do for yourself whenever you can. Copy and post the lists, printed on page 49, to help you keep your mind, body and spirit working for you—not against you!

As I was writing this, I spell-checked the entry, and I had written "girl-fiend" instead of girlfriend for my husband's woman on the side. I think girlfiend is a better description actually. In the opinion of all the Radical Women (and honestly of most other people as well), that's what women are who get emotionally and physically involved with a married man and especially a married man who has a family. So my advice to any woman wondering whether to start a relationship with a married man—don't! (I wanted every reference to a girlfriend in this book spelled the new girlfiend way, but my editor said "No.")

BODY BASICS

Get a physical

Get your teeth cleaned

Get a mammogram

Get a pap smear

Get a bone density test

Get a colonoscopy

BEYOND THE BASICS
When you can afford them

Get a haircut

Get a manicure

Get a pedicure

Get a facial

Get a full-body massage

Get a make-up demonstration

Get a great new outfit

Get a new perfume that says "you"

Light some wonderful candles

Take a luxurious, scented bath

Join a health club

Chapter Two

GET STRONG

In the beginning, being strong was getting to the grocery store and back without crying. Later, it meant realizing I could become my own version of Wonder Woman.

YOU can do that, too!

"When I walked in the bedroom, my husband's girlfriend ran out the back door. I suddenly became Super Woman! I went berserk! I smashed her watch with a cup and flushed her jewelry down the toilet. Then I threw a chair against the plate glass window. My husband was momentarily stunned. I think I actually could have killed him with my bare hands."

A Charter Member of the Radical Women

Being strong comes in many forms. Sometimes extraordinary strength comes in bursts like a person lifting a car in response to an emotional, crisis situation—or becoming 'Superwoman' for a reason like the one above. But a greater challenge is the focus of this chapter—getting strong physically, mentally and emotionally in our normal, everyday circumstances. Of course, physical health and mental and emotional health are inseparable. Most likely, at this point, you are probably feeling emotionally and physically drained and exhausted most of the time—maybe more than you ever have in your entire life. You can change that.

GETTING PHYSICAL AND GETTING HEALTHY

As I've said earlier, when I was in the grip of despair in the middle of this whole mess, I would get on my bike and ride as often as I could. I would ride as fast as I could out in the country on the open road. Some days, I would ride so hard that it was difficult to breathe. It was a challenge to finish. When I got home, I was physically exhausted, but amazingly my mood was better. Set challenges for yourself. Push yourself. Try to walk faster for longer. Do hills. Start running.

My children and their spouses are all athletes with strong, healthy bodies—a great blessing for which I am very thankful. They all participated in school sports, and over the years I saw dozens of great T-shirts with motivational sayings. At one cross country meet, I noticed a neon green shirt that said, "Pain is Weakness Leaving the Body." So true emotionally—not just physically.

Try this. Visualize your weaknesses leaving your body while you are pushing yourself to get stronger. For 30 minutes or an hour or more a day, while your mind is mulling over all your crises, focus on doing laps or working out with weights at a gym or weeding your flower bed or cleaning your basement, or whatever.

At first, I would sometimes cry or pray as I was running on the treadmill. I could get more vocal riding my bike along the open road, which was a great release. For a while, I also listened to a series of motivational tapes while I was at the gym. (But remember, for your safety, no headphones when you are on the road outside!) You'll find that the harder you are pushing yourself physically, the less you will think about your grief and the more you will think about just finishing the ride or the run. That is a good thing!

I also tried a step class that was a complete disaster. Even though I love to dance, the moves demanded too much concentration. I was too distracted. I would end up facing the wrong way or stepping when I should have been lunging or the other way around! When I think about it now, it was pretty comical. Even though the music was great, and the leader said, "It takes a few times to get the hang of this," I never went back.

Next, I tried spinning classes where you and a bunch of other crazy people get on stationary bikes and, with loud pump up music playing, ride as hard as you can for about an hour. The leader tries to kill you by having you spin your legs on the pedals of the bike as fast as you can. I was always one of the older people in the class, and the leader kept looking at me to ask if I was okay. If I'd had the breath, I would have said, "Leave me alone and quit asking me that!" As it was, I just nodded my head.

While everyone else was yelling and getting "in the zone," I was praying that I could survive the 45 minutes without having a heart attack! Of course, no one was holding a gun to my head while I did this, but I didn't want to give middle-agers a bad name, and it got to be a pride thing.

So you don't take unnecessary chances, get a physical before you start anything really crazy. Doing anything physical will get your mind off how terrible your situation is and onto how wonderful your body is. I can promise you, spinning classes will do that!

So, try something new. Yoga. Karate. Fencing. Step aerobics. Stretch your comfort level. Sign up for a class with another Radical Woman or with any friend ready to become lean and mean. Find something you want to try and keep trying until you find a good fit. Don't give up. Exercise that makes you sweat becomes addictive, because you start feeling so much better when you're doing something physically demanding. Try to do something challenging every day. Walk around the block, if nothing else. Cry if you need to. Yell if that helps. Or just thank God for your amazing body and the freedom to use it.

During this time, I made a personal resolution to ring the bell at the top of the rock-climbing wall at a local sporting goods store. My youngest son did it easily. His friends all did it. I looked at them and thought, "I just finished riding my bike across the state; my legs are strong. I can do that." But it was harder than I thought it would be. I tried once and got about halfway up. I kept trying to forget my resolution, but my 14-year-old son would not let me quit—he made me keep trying. And it felt great when I finally did make it and rang the bell! It was a great personal victory.

At the time, my husband and I were separated, not divorced. He said he was trying to end his other relationship, and I thought he was working to get back on track. The day I rang the bell, I stopped by his apartment to tell him about it. His girlfriend was in his apartment when I got there, but I didn't know that at first. She had parked her car somewhere way across the parking lot. My husband definitely didn't want me to come in the apartment, so that made me suspicious, and when my new stronger self barged my way in, there she was. He didn't say anything. She said she had just stopped by for a minute after work. Yeah. Right.

Even though ringing the bell was a huge accomplishment, when I think about that day now, I think mostly about my husband's girlfriend sitting on the couch in her little blue nursing scrubs, and remember how sick at heart I felt. In spite of the heart-wrenching discouragement I felt at the time, I will say that people are still moderately impressed that I actually rang the bell at the climbing wall. I wonder what my husband's girlfriend thought about it.

Defiantly continuing to make yourself get out there helps with self-esteem and improves your self image. (Just don't stop by your husband's apartment after your big victory. Call or celebrate with someone more dependable who really cares about what you accomplished.)

You can read all the books you want about getting fit, you can make all the resolutions you want, but until you really do the work, nothing makes much difference. You certainly won't feel any better unless you make the effort. Set goals. Go to the high school track in the evening and try to improve your time every month. Get serious about getting strong. You will reap not only physical, but emotional, rewards.

I know you probably don't have the energy or even the desire now, but after you have been on your new fitness journey for a while, get on the Internet and explore the possibility of a wilderness/adventure-type vacation. Trips are out there with walking, hiking, or biking programs for every level of fitness. Check out trips for singles if you don't have a friend to go with. You may need to keep this in mind for later. It's probably better if you're past the sobbing stage before you sign up.

In the meantime, remind yourself that you alone are responsible for how you feel. No one else will keep you healthy. That's your job. Doctors, nutritionists, personal trainers, life coaches, massage therapists and counselors can all give advice. But in the end, it's up to you to keep yourself healthy. You have to make the decision. You have to have the discipline. Think of yourself as an elite athlete, because in reality, that's what your best self is, and that is what we can all become. No matter what shape we are in now, we can improve it.

Visualize yourself with a new stronger, leaner, healthier, more capable body. Women our age and older run triathlons and marathons, bike across their states, run in charity races, master new skills. There has never been a better or more appropriate time to start training than now. Say to yourself,

"This is my body! This is my life! No one else is going to destroy me or my life. I won't let them!" And mean it. By taking physical control, the emotional ups and downs smooth out a little and become easier to handle, too.

Everybody needs to practice good habits for staying physically healthy. You know them already, but the list below will be a reminder. You can copy the list and post it in your kitchen. Below, we will talk about these habits in more detail.

THE TOP TEN HEALTHY HABITS FOR
Radical Women

1. **DRINK** 6-8 glasses of water every day.

2. **EAT** 2.5 cups of vegetables and 1.5 cups of fruit daily.

3. **STAY AWAY FROM** high-calorie, high fat or high sugar foods.

4. **SHOP** Healthy.

5. **TAKE** a multi-vitamin and mineral supplement daily.

6. **EAT WHOLE GRAINS** and fiber as needed.

7. **GET PLENTY** of fresh air and sunshine.

8. **GET PLENTY** of rest.

9. **WATCH YOUR** alcohol consumption.

10. **DEAL WITH** your depression.

Top Ten Healthy Habits

1. DRINK 6-8 glasses of water every day—you know you should. As the ads say, "Just do it." In fact, go get yourself a glass of water right now. Water helps every single system in your body—skin, hair, digestion, and everything else you can think of. I got a funky, fun goblet to keep on my desk to encourage myself to drink water. A big, plastic water bottle to sip from all day is just as good, and maybe better, because you know exactly how much you've had. Remember, too, that coffee, tea and sodas do not count toward your daily requirement. These drinks act as diuretics and actually lower the amount of water in your body.

A nurse at the hospital where my mom was being treated for dehydration said that new research shows that your body responds to even healthy liquids in a different way than it responds to water. Your body sees orange juice as a food. Water is the only water. Drink more and you'll discover your skin will look better. You'll feel better. Your digestion will be better. Make sure you are drinking enough water every day.

2. EAT 2.5 cups of veggies and 1.5 cups of fruit every day. And if you exercise more than 30 minutes a day, you need more. According to a *Wall Street Journal* article on nutrition, the ten top most nutritious fruits and vegetables are: spinach, romaine lettuce, broccoli, tomatoes, bell peppers, cantaloupe, tangerines, blueberries, apricots and raspberries.

Eat a rainbow of choices every day. Different colors have different nutrients, and the more variety the better. Research from many sources shows that the simple act of eating at least five different fruits or vegetables a day makes a person considerably more healthy and have a longer life expectancy.

We've all known that eating breakfast is good for us, too. Didn't you tell your children that for years? People who eat fruit at breakfast are healthier as well. The *Wall Street Journal* article continued, "People who eat fruits and vegetables more than three times a day reduce their risk of having a stroke and dying from cardiovascular disease by nearly a quarter, compared with those who eat them less than once a day, according to an American Journal of Clinical Nutrition study."

Eating more fruits and veggies may also be one of the best ways to lose weight, and high consumption of produce may improve bone health which is especially good for women in our age group. Scientists also say it's better to eat an actual fruit or vegetable rather than take a pill containing its nutrients. And we should also concentrate on eating dark green veggies as well as the lighter ones. The study confirmed that frozen or canned vegetables are almost as beneficial as raw or steamed. Use this time of personal transition to fine-tune your eating habits. It will do wonders for your overall feeling of well-being!

3. Stop eating high calorie, high fat or high sugar foods to help you forget how discouraged or sad you feel. Try, if you possibly can, to think about how what you eat will affect you over the long haul. The seduction of unhealthy, high-calorie, high fat or high sugar food is in how good they taste right this minute. It's okay *occasionally* to get away from the pain for an instant by eating a candy bar. Sometimes it's worth it. But consider how you want to look and feel in a year and decide if what you want to eat now will help you get there.

If you find yourself constantly *overeating*, here are some quick guides to regulate your portions. One serving of meat is the size of a deck of cards. One ounce of cheese is about the size of two dice. One serving of rice, potatoes or pasta is about one-half cup. Most Americans eat way too much, mostly out of habit.

4. Shop Healthy. To eat foods that are bad for you, you must have them around. Make a copy of the grocery list on the right to take with you the next time you go to the store. Shop healthy, and keep healthy foods and snacks on hand.

The Radical Woman's
TOP TEN GROCERY LIST

1. **Fresh fruits and vegetables.** Fresh produce has more nutrients per calorie than any other food. For highest potency, they should be juiced, eaten raw, or lightly steamed.

2. **Dairy products** like yogurt, milk and cottage cheese. Buy plain, low-fat, sugar-free varieties that are free of artificial sweeteners. Add your own fruit for flavor.

3. **Canola or olive oil.** Use in cooking and salad dressings.

4. **Dried beans, lentils, and black-eyed peas.** Precooked varieties may also be used for convenience. Combine with rice for an even more power-filled nutritional benefit.

6. **Raw nuts.** Especially almonds, walnuts and hazelnuts.

7. **Whole-grain pastas, breads, and snacks.** If it doesn't say "whole" on the ingredient listing, as in "whole wheat flour" or "whole durham flour," it isn't. Fiber is crucial to any healthy eating plan.

8. **Tea.** Drink a variety of flavored teas that do not contain sugar or artificial sweeteners.

9. **Salsa.** Use as a replacement for sugar-laden ketchup or dips.

10. **Herbs and spices.** Including garlic, ginger, thyme, rosemary, basil, cayenne pepper and turmeric. For more flavor and better health, use more spices and less butter and salt.

5. Take a multivitamin and mineral supplement. When your life is in turmoil, especially, start your day with a multivitamin and mineral supplement. It's more important now than ever. When you are under the terrible strain and stress of marital problems and divorce, you may forget to eat or lose your appetite. Taking a vitamin guarantees that you get the nutrients you need. Or, you may be eating junk food because you feel out of control. A daily vitamin helps in that case, too.

6. Eat whole grains and fiber. Most Americans eat only one-third of the fiber they need. Increasing intake of fiber is one of the simplest and most important things we can do to improve our health. Think—and eat—whole grains. I know some diet plans focus on low carbs, but try to get enough fiber in the carbs you do eat. Make fiber a priority.

7. Get plenty of fresh air and sunshine. When we are in the great outdoors—even just walking around the block—we usually breathe more deeply, and the sun improves our mood. Even if it's raining or cold, being in the elements has a way of activating our senses. Take deep, full breaths. Take a little more time on the exhale than you do on the inhale. Remember your sunscreen!

If you are walking outside, lift your arms up above your head as you inhale. Move them slowly back to your sides with your exhale. Stand up straight. Walk boldly with confidence with your head up, your back straight. I like the verse from Colossians that says: "Don't shuffle along, eyes to the ground, absorbed with the things right in front of you." Act as if you feel sure, confident, and in control. Smile. If you can, walk with a trusted friend who will let you talk about your situation. Talk about the good things in your life—and there are many. You are trying to figure out how to deal with some awful things, and discussing them can be helpful, but remember to ask your friend how *her* life is going, and *be interested.*

When you go get coffee or are having lunch, ask for a table outside. Feel the sun and the breeze and enjoy the fresh air. Even if it's snowing, put on your boots and get outside.

For several years when my children were young, I walked most school days with two or three friends. We bragged that even if the wind chill was 40 degrees below zero, we did our morning walk and even made angels in the snow! Go sledding with your grandkids. Shovel your driveway yourself. It will be good for your body and your psyche, and it will save you a little money as well. Rake the leaves in the fall. Plant new flowers or a garden in the spring. Just get outside and thank God for every single ability you have that you can enjoy in the out-of-doors.

In Aleksandr I. Solzhenitsyn's incredible book *The Gulag Archipelago*, the prisoners often waited all day for one little shaft of sunlight to come into their cell. They would stand joyously in that shaft of light following it across the cell until it disappeared, which took less than half an hour. That book made me appreciate every single little joy available in the free, potential-filled day-to-day life like ours, even with our heartbreak, disappointments and temporary defeats. Read that book to put things in a bigger per-spective. Don't take the quiet, everyday pleasures of life for granted. Be thankful that you can experience them. People all over the world, as well as in your neighborhood, are suffering and struggling with life and death issues every single day.

"Don't take the quiet, everyday pleasures of life for granted. Be thankful that you can experience them."

Last year our book club read *Reading Lolita in Tehran*, a book about women in Iran. The book tells the story of a teacher and her students who secretly, and at the risk of their lives, meet and read forbidden Western literature. The book taught me to take no freedom for granted, even the simple privilege of walking around unencumbered by a long, black burka. Don't take the clear, unmuffled sounds of the cicadas and the feel of the warm sun and the cool breeze on your skin for granted. Be aware of those exquisite everyday sensations.

8. Get plenty of rest. Easier said than done, I know. All the Radical Women felt like emotional wrecks and physical zombies during much of our crisis because we weren't getting quality sleep. Lack of sleep affects everything else you are trying to do, of course. It makes you irritable, grumpy, emotional and just plain exhausted.

Learning to sleep alone is hard. It is common to suffer from irregular sleep patterns, to have trouble falling asleep and to wake up early. Such signs may signal depression. If you wake up regularly at least an hour before your usual time, and feel especially hopeless and despairing when you do, depression is a likely culprit. All the Radical Women had trouble sleeping, and you will too, most likely. Try to keep a reasonable schedule. Don't drink caffeine or alcohol before bed, and don't exercise strenuously just before you turn in. Take a nap if you need to, but not later than 3 in the afternoon. I would often stay up until midnight or later, and my normal—affair and divorce—wake-up time was about 4 a.m. Years later, I feel like I'm still catching up on rest.

Some personal reflections about sleep: In the beginning of our separation, I would try sleeping in different spots in our king-sized bed. I would try sleeping on his side and my side and in the middle. It reminded me of the movie "Something's Gotta Give." Diane Keaton's character said she had hit a milestone when she could finally sleep in the middle of the bed. In reality, especially in the beginning, nothing much helped no matter where we tried to sleep.

After the divorce was final, I was still trying to find a place I could really relax and sleep. I bought my own new double bed to replace our king-sized bed. It didn't seem so much as if there should be two people sleeping in it. I got an old weathered iron farm gate and put it against the wall as a headboard, and I put little white Christmas lights on it. I bought several wonderful quilts, one for each season. I loved the bed, and the mattress was perfect. But still, sleep was elusive. And I hardly ever turned on the Christmas lights. Somehow that seemed too frivolous.

In the beginning, when our son was spending the night at his father's, or later, after he was away at college (I'm wondering if this sounds too weird to tell), when I was physically overcome with loneliness and grief, I would occasionally sleep in his bed just to feel closer to him—just to smell him on his pillow and feel him in the room. (Freud would have a field day with this I'm sure, and I sort of hesitate to admit it!) I think since our youngest was the only one at home during the affair, the separations and finally the divorce, it seemed even more sad and lonely when he was gone. I was ready for him to experience more independence, and he definitely was ready for it, but I missed him. I missed his youthful optimism. I missed his playing the piano. I missed his friends. But most of all I just missed him—his presence, his natural, unintended, youthful encouragement, his adventurous personality.

Our other children were 30, 28, 26 and on their own already. It's always hard when one of your children leaves for college, but the last one probably brings the most intense feeling of separation—especially if your husband has flown the coop, as well.

By this time, I had bought a new house for my son and me with a kitchen and family room all together. I tried sleeping on a little love seat in front of the fireplace in that new family room. It was a small space with a comfortable, overstuffed love seat. I am about 5'3" tall, and I could just about stretch out, but not quite, so I usually slept a little curled up with a big family quilt over me. It was a great sofa for a good book, and on nights when I just couldn't face going into my bedroom alone and getting into that cold bed by myself, I would sleep on that love seat usually reading until I dozed off. Sometimes I made a fire in the fireplace, and we would both be cold by morning.

I even tried sleeping in a sleeping bag on the sun porch with all of the windows open. Nothing helped really but time. I had been sleeping with another human being for 33 years. And, I have cold feet. Since the day we married, I had slept with nothing on. (My two sexy honeymoon negligees got about one minute's wear each.) It just seemed how it should be—body to body—skin to skin. I loved it, and my husband's body was always warm.

When I was sleeping alone, I felt naked instead of natural with nothing on, and my feet were always freezing. Sleeping alone in the winter, I would often end up putting on a sweat suit or something flannel and socks. I would even need an extra blanket. But I still felt cold.

The only thing the Radical Women can advise about sleep is to try different things and see what works best for you. Probably nothing will work very well, especially in the beginning.

In my notebook, I kept a picture of a beautiful woman stretched out on her stomach under the covers in a luxurious bed—sleeping peacefully. I tried to be like that. I tried to get that contented "sleeping by myself" feeling in my bed. I usually wasn't very successful. After a while, though, there actually were nights I enjoyed spreading out and having the whole bed to myself. But that was much, much later. A friend of mine keeps a big, somewhat overpoweringly tedious book by the bed to read until sleep takes over.

I tried books, but if they had anything romantic in them, I'd cry. I often read the Bible because it was transcendent and truthful, and it would give me some deeper thought to ponder instead of mulling over the latest devastating betrayal or worry. I would often repeat a favorite verse or chapter as a mantra of encouragement or protection. Anything to give me hope and dispel the agonizing darkness I was feeling. The familiar 23rd Psalm was a favorite. Sometimes I would think about only one phrase or one line: "The Lord is my shepherd. I shall not want. … He restores my soul." I often repeated my verse for the year—whatever it was. The first year my verse was from 2 Samuel: "It is God who arms me with strength and makes my way perfect." Write down a verse and keep it by the bed and read it first thing in the morning and the last thing at night. Memorize it. Believe it. Those words helped as much as anything to quiet my heart.

9. Watch your alcohol consumption. Okay, here's the deal about alcohol: It's a depressant, and the last thing we need right now is another depressant. Our husbands, their girlfriends and their actions are more than enough of a depressant for anyone! The fact is, alcohol can make us feel better only in the short term. You may think it makes you sleep better. You may think it makes things seem not so bad. But after the buzz wears off, you still have the problem, and you have a headache, and you are sluggish and it takes more effort to get going.

During the time of your separation and divorce, alcohol is a handy, accessible crutch. It is very easy to become dependent on it. I know even for me—the embarrassing Carrie Nation to all of our kids and their friends when they were teenagers—alcohol could have become a problem. I started having a glass of wine with dinner almost every night when our son wasn't home. I didn't want him to see me drinking every night, because I didn't want him to think alcohol is a solution to personal problems. But when I was sitting in the kitchen alone, a glass of wine or two was hard to resist.

I think an occasional drink or glass of wine is okay. I think being drunk any time is wrong. I grew up in a family that used little or no alcohol. Both scripture and experience point to the folly and often disastrous consequences of drinking too much. So, even though I have done my share of espousing the dangers of alcohol to all of our children, I'll admit, on the days our youngest was not home, I almost always had wine with dinner. I love the taste of good red wine. I was also reading articles in respected publications that said a glass of red wine is actually good for your health, so I had no trouble rationalizing doing that. And a glass of wine made my simple meal of cheese, fruit and bread, or chips and salsa, or popcorn, taste that much better. There were a few nights when I had more than one glass, and I thought to myself, "I'm doing this because I like it, not because I need it," but I knew in reality that I was on the edge of this becoming more than an innocent glass of wine every night.

I never drank a whole bottle in one day, but I drank half a bottle on a few occasions. That is not a good decision for anyone, particularly someone short who is under a lot of emotional stress, or who is sad, or who wants to escape the depressing details of trying to survive. That is not a good road to head down. But almost all the Radical Women were tempted at least in the beginning. Plus, the risk of making a late night, wine-induced, emotional call to your former spouse is a possibility, too. The Radical Women agree that those calls were universally disastrous.

And while I'm confessing my almost nightly glasses of wine, I will come clean about something else. Some days definitely are worse than others during your journey through divorce. Just expect them. One day like that came after my divorce had been final for more than two years. My business was steadily growing. I was gaining confidence. I was looking healthy and fit. I was finally getting back on my feet.

Then out of the blue, the week before Christmas, my ex-husband called to say he was marrying his new girlfriend. And he called at 6:30 in the morning! I was working out at the health club at the time, so I called him back, and he told me the news. I learned later that he had told the children the night before, and they said he should tell me before I heard it from someone else. So he called at 6:30 the next morning to tell me the good news. Trying to sound aloof, I told him I hoped he would be happy, but I hoped he had learned some things over the last few years. I wanted to tell him, "I think you've done despicable, selfish, horrible things and have broken not only every promise you made to me but have destroyed the confidence of our children and I hope your penis turns black and falls off and you get some terrible disease and you're miserable every day of your life!" But I didn't.

I just hung up the phone and cried pretty much the rest of the day. All the children either called or came over that day to give me a little extra support, I think. When each one came over or called, quiet tears would start all over again. I couldn't help it. Our oldest son brought coffee from Starbucks and a new CD for me. They all conveyed their love and reassured me that everything would be okay. I love them all more than they will ever understand, and I especially appreciated their encouragement and comfort on that particularly difficult day.

That same day, one of my biggest and oldest clients called to say they were changing direction as far as marketing was concerned. I had already considered and even suggested ending that business relationship, and it was really time for that. The change was good for both of us for a lot of reasons, but the timing was terrible. And they ended it instead of me. The call came on Friday the week before Christmas, and I was worried about the loss of income for the holidays.

Then, a few hours later, my doctor called and said the results of my mammogram came back with something weird going on, and I was going to need a breast biopsy—"No immediate urgency, but we may as well go ahead and get it done on Tuesday." All of those things happened on the same day.

I'm telling you this because that afternoon I was making a fancy new cake for Christmas dinner, and the cake was supposed to sit for about a week soaking in bourbon. I was already emotional enough, and the call about my breast biopsy came during the afternoon when I was finishing up this cake. I had a pint of bourbon from the liquor store for the recipe sitting right on the counter.

For some reason, after I hung up the phone with the doctor's office, I thought about the cowboys in old Westerns who would take a bottle of "hooch" out of their saddlebag and take a big swig with a flourish. Well, I did exactly that. I put the bottle up to my lips and put my head back like in the movies, and took a big gulp. It was strong going down and tasted terrible, but I'll admit it left a soft puddle of warmth in the pit of my stomach. No one was there to share the moment, but later I told my kids and laughed about what they would've thought had they come in the back door and seen their mother taking a big chug out of a bottle of cheap bourbon. I'm not sure they would have believed me if I had told them it was the first time I had ever done that. Well, it was, and, so far, I haven't done it since.

In looking back, I guess my kids knew deep down that I would never let myself get addicted to alcohol after all the grief I had given them about drinking. The first year of my husband's affair, our kids had a birthday party for me—just a quiet dinner at my daughter's apartment. They had prepared a wonderful dinner, baked chicken with all the trimmings, and had gone together to buy me a bottle of tequila—sort of as a joke, I think. For some reason, at the time it was a perfect gift from them to me, because it seems they were trying to say in an offhand, humorous way, "We know this is a terrible time for you. We know how awful this is for you. This calls for extreme measures—your very own bottle of Cuervo Gold." It also said to me, "We know you will use this wisely and sparingly." I'm pretty sure they felt confident that they would never come in the house and find me in a drunken stupor lying on the couch! They didn't know, however, how easy it would be on some lonely nights to think, "I don't want to deal with this," and just drink the whole bottle all at once.

10. Deal with your depression. I remember the counselor drawing a picture on the erasable board in his office—a picture of two sections of nerves between which nothing was connecting. "It's an electrical imbalance," he said. "It's a chemical imbalance. It doesn't have anything to do with your ability to cope with this situation. It has to do with the effects of sadness and stress on your system, and if it gets too serious or lasts too long, those connections cannot be made without some help. You need to be on antidepressants," he said. I started to cry again. There was definitely a period when I was having a hard time getting through the days in a normal way.

I cried all the time. On this particular day, I remember finding out that my husband had been lying to me every single day for more than two months. We had started—again—to rebuild our relationship on the first of January— a fresh start. We were going to try—again—to make this work. He was going to do his part; I was going to do mine. I found out three days after Valentine's Day, that during this time he had either seen or talked to his girlfriend every single day since January first, even when he was out of town.

He had given her daffodils, a heart-shaped box and other gifts on Valentine's Day. Meanwhile, we had been living in the same house. We had been sleeping together. I had been trying to redevelop trust and not wonder where his heart was while we were lying in the same bed. And he had lied to me every single day. He would say things like, "How will this ever work if you won't trust me?" Or, "I said I'm sorry. Why can't you get over this and move on?"

On the day I found out, I just lost it. That's the day the counselor said, "I think it's time for some help." Even though I didn't want to be on medicine, the counselor called my internist, and the two of them decided I needed to be on a very low dose of something. I didn't even think about mentioning to my doctor that I was taking some vitamin and herbal supplements that were natural and basically harmless. What I didn't know was that some of those supplements and antidepressants don't mix.

I remember taking our youngest to piano lessons shortly after I began the medicine. I started feeling woozy and dizzy. By the time I got to the lesson I was throwing up everything I had ever eaten, and I felt absolutely, unbelievably sick. I called my friend the doctor, and, after a few questions, he figured out what was going on. On the phone, I was crying and throwing up and felt so bad that I thought I might actually die. He called my family in Wichita, and my older brother was at my house before morning.

Even though I probably should have, the doctors didn't make me take any more antidepressants. I said it was an instant cure. I thought if I didn't pull myself together I would have to take another one of those pills, and I might die before the day was over!

I know antidepressants can be very helpful during times of loss and stress. I just didn't want to take them. I don't like to take medicine of any kind, and for me it seemed like a cop-out. I thought I would rather struggle and cry my way through this with a clear head and not be drugged. I also thought, "I have God."

"That's the day the counselor said, 'I think it's time for some help.'"

I had brazenly told people to "trust God and he will see you through anything." I have learned that having God doesn't eliminate real emotional struggles. And antidepressants can be a help and benefit. As for me, I think I was afraid I might become zombie-like. I wanted to handle this on my own. I was afraid if I didn't experience the whole awful agony of this, and rise above it, that I would never have faced it, really. I think you just have to get through some things, as ugly and hard as the process is. Some grief you simply have to endure until you figure out how to get through it. I concluded, "If I take something to make this sadness go away artificially, I will never really deal with it." It's not a weakness or a spiritual failure to use antidepressants. I just ridiculously, stubbornly didn't want to. In reality, I might have recovered more easily and more quickly had I used them as my counselor and doctor wanted me to.

From other women I have talked to, I've learned that if used correctly antidepressants can be very helpful—even life-changing. They can help reestablish chemical connections, and are nothing to be embarrassed or ashamed about. I also think antidepressants can be a godsend to help you face your situation, but with a little more reason, and a little less physical and emotional agony. You will have to discuss the options with your counselor or physician and figure out the best choice for you.

Balance is the Key

In America, we believe that if a little is good, more is better. Obviously that is not true. Try to cultivate a strong, steady progression to your goals. Don't try to do everything at once. Take baby steps. Set reasonable goals and work toward them with determination. Be persistent—but patient. The good will come. The strength will come. The power will come. But those things won't happen all at once. It's a process—a lifelong process that will bring positive results from the very first moment, but can also provide us with big enough goals for a lifetime.

We need a personal standard of wellness that is balanced and life-affirming and that has healthy strategies we can adhere to our whole lives. Trying to stay emotionally-centered and balanced during this turmoil is difficult, but it becomes progressively easier if we make the commitment to do something toward our goals every day.

CHAPTER THREE

ORGANIZE THE CHAOS

Just because your life is a disaster
of disorder and despair right now
doesn't mean they won't shut off
your lights and add on
a ridiculous late fee if you
don't pay your bill on time.

This chapter is hard for me to write because, I'll admit right off the bat, I am not an organized person. I want to be more organized. I try to be. I'm getting better. But I still have trouble throwing things away. I save cards and letters from important people in my life. I save interesting articles and store past projects I've done for clients. I put things in stacks instead of files like I should. But even though I'm not naturally organized, I keep reminding myself that I have accomplished lots of worthwhile things in my life in spite of it. I am proud of all of those accomplishments, and when I start to beat myself up about my failures in the area of organization, I try to give myself credit for things I'm good at.

Nonetheless, I have to confess there are more times than I want to admit when I cannot put my hands on something I need immediately, or in some cases, ever. In fact, occasionally I have to make a call to get another copy. Sometimes I have to pay a penalty because I'm late with a payment. I have even had to go to the bank and close out one account and open a brand new one because my records were so messed up. My life would be much easier and much less stressful if I had the self-discipline to throw more stuff away and to always keep things in their proper places. But like I said, we all have weaknesses, so take pride in your strong suits and try to improve the others. Don't lose sleep over those areas that are less than perfect. Just keep diligently moving forward, and pray that your family will be patient—and your electricity stays on!

One of the life benefits of this cataclysmic event is that it has forced me to become more organized. It was absolutely imperative to do so. And even though on some days I still feel very far from where I need to be, at least I am moving in the right direction.

I used to count on my husband to keep track of all the important stuff. Birth certificates. Wills. Titles. Insurance papers. Financial records. Investment documents. Warranties. Records. Now I have to do that myself. If you are a naturally organized, orderly person, keep it up! I'm envious. But remember, it will take extra effort to maintain that level of control in the middle of all the confusion and disarray during a divorce.

All of us in the Radical group were at times so distracted by the turmoil in our emotional lives, that it was often hard to keep track of even the most elemental things. That's why I included sticky notes in the original folder I gave to the Radical Recovery group. However, I knew without a doubt that I had to go beyond surface measures like sticky notes and make some significant, serious changes in my life.

Start with Decluttering

When you are faced with life after divorce, there are several areas where organization becomes mandatory. For me, the key beginning task was to declutter. Get rid of stuff. Get rid of extraneous, broken down, unnecessary stuff. During the last few years I have done a lot toward that goal. I've had to. For one thing, my living space has been reduced drastically. It's way smaller. I have sent truckloads of usable household items, furniture and appliances to the helping ministry at church and to Goodwill and to any other organization that would pick them up. (But remember this unspoken law of the universe: whenever you set things out by the curb for pickup, expect rain that day. It never fails.) I have had two garage sales during all of this, and I have also made a pledge to never have another one as long as I live. I will just put everything out by the driveway with a sign that says, "Free! Please take this stuff!" if I have to. I have given everything I can to my children.

I still have a long way to go, but I am an eternal optimist, and I have hope that I will finally get there. Just writing this section gives me a fresh determination to keep on keeping on. My accountant once told me, "It's a process, not a project" when he was helping me with my taxes. I try to remember that concept in other areas of my life—like decluttering, organizing and maintaining order.

Most of the Radical Women went through the "cleaning, scrubbing, ordering stage" of grieving. This stage of the process gives you something to do that is physically demanding, but in most cases pretty mindless. And it gives you some small sense of control over something. I cleaned out closets, cabinets, the basement and lots of other areas as well. A counselor told me that this "ordering" phase was also why I suddenly started doing the crossword puzzle in the paper everyday. It is so neat and tidy, and it consumes your mind for the time it takes to do it. You have a sense of control while the rest of your life is spinning wildly in every direction.

The counselor said that many people confronting stressful, life-changing situations often almost absentmindedly start doing things, anything, to get any sense of structure back into their lives—even if it's organizing the silverware drawer.

Decluttering can also mean getting rid of the trash and junk in your emotional life. Bitterness, fear, malice, worry and countless other negative emotions take up valuable time and energy that could be used on more productive pursuits. What good does bitterness do? What purpose does pessimism serve? How is obsessive worry helping you live your life to its fullest? A certain amount of anger and concern can help you get where you need to be, but excessive anger, fear and worry will do nothing more than keep you in a state of turmoil and eliminate any real delight.

Being stuck in the negatives makes progress on any front less likely. So to begin with, try to get as much physical and emotional junk out of your life as possible. Once you do that, you begin to find a welcome sense of freedom and release.

DIVIDING UP THE PROPERTY

If you have not yet gone through and separated your household stuff from your husband's, that's a whole truckload of pain and heartbreak that has to be faced. But once it's done, it's done, and you can begin to let things go, physically and mentally. The day my husband and I were to separate our household belongings was agony for me. In fact, the first time we tried to do it, I started crying and said, "I can't do this today. I just can't handle this today," so we set

RADICAL RECOVERY

another date. I eventually had to face the reality of that day, as much as I tried to forestall it.

We set the ground rules for dividing our household property, as it's called in the Divorce Decree. Anything that was an outright gift to him or to me would go to that person. We also decided that any family pieces—almost entirely his, even though I am the one who retrieved them—went to him. On the day of reckoning, we went through every room in our house, each saying what we wanted and negotiating on the rest. We are talking about 33 plus years of accumulated physical belongings representing our life together. Dishes. Silverware. Crystal. Furniture. The piano. Baseball cards. Art. The stereo. The television. Books. Music. Kitchen stuff. Every little thing you acquire as you live and raise four kids together. It was an exhausting, agonizing, lump-in-your-throat, pain-in-your-chest, terrible day.

The hardest part for me was dealing with the sentimental pieces we had bought or made together throughout our married life. Artwork. Special holiday things. Gifts to both of us. We had been advised that the easiest way to do this was to have one person choose a thing, then have the other person choose another thing, and so on. I had already specifically asked our children if there were any pieces they wanted, so when my turn came to choose, I got those first to pass along immediately to them. After those pieces were taken care of, difficulties came up on several items.

I had found these great 5-feet-tall Halloween witches that we got for each of our children, and we got one for us, too. He picked that (before we even got to the holiday stuff, which I thought was unfair!), and I still miss that witch when Halloween rolls around. I am going to find one to replace her. Another point of contention was the original printing plate for the front page of our newspaper the morning of the first moonwalk. I was working at the local newspaper in the advertising art department during that momentous time, so I got the printing plate and had it framed. Well, my husband wanted that, but since I was the one working there and got it, I thought it should be mine. He disagreed.

He also took a sentimental Christmas numbered print that my Dad had given to each of his children and their families. I thought that should be mine. The last thing was a great, framed poster of all different kinds of trout that some good friends had given me when I graduated from college in 1995—I love to fish. My ex-husband didn't remember that they had given it to me, and he wanted it. He is very persistent, and I just didn't have the emotional energy to argue very hard. Not long after that day, I discovered that our middle son had quietly taken several of the objects in question and put them in my stash of stuff. His father made some protestations to this child, but apparently not many, and never said a word to me about it.

In truth, going through the stuff, reliving the memories, dealing with the heartache of divvying up all of the accumulated possessions was harder than I thought. The son of one of the Radical Women said he went home from work that night and told his wife, "I'll do anything. I'll do whatever you want. I just don't want to ever have to go through separating our things like that." In the end, despite the immediate trauma, as both of my brothers said, "It's just stuff."

They were right, and since that day I have even parted on my own with several items I fought to keep. At the time, though, each piece in question seemed to have some special emotion-filled significance to me. They represented physical pieces of our life together that I hated to give up. Even though "it all ends up on the curb," as a speaker pointed out at church a few weeks ago, at the moment you're tempted to put your arms around all of that stuff and try desperately to hold on because you think those touchable, tangible belongings might somehow keep your life from flying apart. They don't.

> *"…at the moment you're tempted to put your arms around all of that stuff and try desperately to hold on because you think those touchable, tangible belongings might somehow keep your life from flying apart."*

By default I ended up with all of the family pictures. Most of them were in boxes in the basement and just never came up in the dividing process. This is one of the things we talked about at our first Radical meeting. What do you do with all of those pictures? What happens to the big family portrait that hung over our fireplace. What about the big family pictures we had taken on the ski slopes every year? Or the black-and-white portraits of my husband and me taken by a wonderful photographer friend every year on our travel group trip? What do you do with all of those pictures? Ours are still in the basement carefully protected in a big black plastic bag.

Most of the small family photographs were not very organized, and I could never make myself go through those boxes of pictures. It made me too sad. My only—and very organized—daughter took all that lifetime of pictures, went through them, separated them into categories and put them neatly in photo boxes with labels on the front. Family. Wyoming. Vacations. New House. Friends. Holidays. Trips. To this day, I have not been able to go through those pictures. Maybe someday I will, or maybe after my ex-husband and I are both gone our children will have to figure out what to do with them.

Soon after all the selections were made about who got what, I found a wonderful, warm, but much smaller, house for our youngest child and me. But that meant getting rid of more things. And we knew the deadline for the old house to be completely cleared out. I still had my part of 33 years of accumulated kids' toys, sports equipment, garden tools, junk. My ex-husband was living in an apartment at this time, so most of the undecided odds and ends stayed with me in the house by default. I picked out a weekend that was convenient for all of our children and said, "This is the weekend. Be here if you want to collect your boxes, and if you want to have anything to say about all of this other stuff." We had the Great Family Clean-Out Weekend!

The kids were all more aggressive at putting things in the giveaway or garage sale piles than I was. More than a few times, I would go retrieve things from those two piles and put them in my undecided pile.

The day was still hard, but having us all there doing the sorting together made it much easier and even occasionally fun and funny. At one point my six-year-old granddaughter and I went through the laundry room with all of its storage shelves full of wrapping paper, craft supplies, sewing stuff, kids puzzle magazines and such. Our mantra became "When in doubt, Toss it out!"—something I had read in one of my dozens of books on organization. Having her bright happy presence in that room with me made the ordeal so much easier to face. In fact, she made it fun.

The weekend was exhausting, but liberating. The huge task was so much easier to handle as a group, with each of us bolstering the others and knowing that we were making the best of it. One helpful bit of advice is this: Have the piles of things you are giving away or throwing away picked up as soon as possible. I kept looking out at the driveway and having the urge to bring something or other back into my house.

Whatever method works for you, do it. And remember, "It's all just stuff." In reality, you will gain a sense of release and freedom by getting rid of things that clutter your space in your house and in your mind. I know you don't think so now, but before long, you won't miss 99 percent of that stuff you want to hold on to.

Also, the few days before moving day, my younger brother and his family generously came to help us pack. Without my knowing, this brother placed a frantic call that first night to my older brother saying, "Get Mom and Dad and anyone else you can and get up here! We need help!" What a huge job!

We had boxes and boxes of stuff even after the Great Clean-Out Weekend. Having so many of my family helping us made the job so much more pleasant than if my high-school son and I had tried to do this enormous job by ourselves. My oldest son even turned around on his way to work that day and came back to help. All I know is that I never would have made it without my family. There was lots of joking and laughing about all of my belongings, and my family's light-hearted jabs made me realize that I had way too many things. Every day it was easier to say, "I don't need these old ski boots, or whatever, taking up space in my life!" Too, there was so much work to do that I didn't have time to be sad, and we were all totally exhausted by moving day.

I remember well the evening before moving day. It was a gorgeous evening, and we set up an eight-foot long folding table on the back deck. The leaves on the trees were that bright summer green, and all was still and beautiful. We were tired and dirty, and we ordered pizza with all the trimmings. We had soft drinks, opened a couple of bottles of wine and enjoyed a wonderful meal together. We laughed at the enormity of the job we had done. We congratulated ourselves at how much we had accomplished. We had a *great* time.

My extended family turned something that could have been very traumatic into a celebration of togetherness. All the while, at the same time, my husband was in his study, sorting and loading up his books, papers and belongings by himself while we were all laughing, talking and enjoying the meal. He later complained, "You had all those people helping you. I had to do all of that by myself." I'll have to admit, I have an absolutely extraordinary family, but not one of them felt very sorry for my ex-husband that evening. We had more than enough of our own to do anyway. As far as we were concerned, he wanted a new woman and a new life—and he could pack for himself.

GUARDING YOUR PHYSICAL SAFETY

This Organize the Chaos section deals not only with basic paring down and organization but with safety issues as well. Physical safety becomes more critical for us now. The simple act of making sure your doors are locked is important. My husband used to always do that. Now, I have to remember to do it myself. Be careful talking in public about living alone. Be cautious. Make sure that if you leave some place after dark, you have a friend — a Radical Woman or anyone—to call to report that you got home safely.

When I was first divorced and went on my first trip by myself, I realized that I had no one to call to say I got there in one piece. I could have called my children, and they often checked on me, but there was not one person who was specifically waiting to hear if I made the trip all right. Facing that fact made me feel unbelievably lonely and depressed. Coming home on the plane by myself was just as hard, and I hated walking to my car by myself and driving home in a snowstorm by myself and coming into a dark and quiet house with no one waiting for me to get home. The dog wasn't even there. I remember sitting on a stool in the kitchen, looking around and realizing that I didn't have anyone to tell about my trip and wondering if I was going to feel that soundless ache for the rest of my life. You are probably asking yourself some variation of that, too. Try to be patient. This stage is worse than terrible, but it does not last forever.

Travel seems easier when one of you can wait with the luggage while the other one gets the car or whatever. One of the first purchases I made after my divorce was a smallish suitcase on rollers. I knew I would be carrying my suitcase myself, so I needed something I could easily get from here to there. But even with that, traveling alone is one more thing you have to adjust to. It's difficult at first like everything else, but eventually, in tiny increments it gets easier.

When I was in college and had to travel home or anywhere else, I looked forward to the journey, because at that time it was an adventure. I always met interesting people in the airport or on the plane. The sensations now can be just the same. Our experience often depends on how we perceive it. Instead of dreading the trip, try to find something good about it. Smile. Be friendly. Cultivate your adventurous spirit. I spent the first couple of trips on the plane looking out the window mostly and trying not to cry. Get a good book. Buy some current magazines. Try the crossword puzzle.

Traveling alone will get easier, but it takes time for that to happen and probably longer than you think it should. At least try to realize that each one of these excursions that you survive and conquer is another step to becoming more secure in who you are and in your abilities to learn and grow. But I also know that right now it brings loneliness, heartache and a yearning to share those things with your ex-husband. That is not going to happen. That relationship is gone. He has moved on, so you are going to have to figure out how to do so as well.

Not only do you need to be careful at home and when you are traveling, but you also must be very careful in your use of the Internet. You are probably not into Internet dating at this point, and you may never be, but be cautious about giving out your telephone number, address or social security number to anyone.

It may seem silly to remind you, but don't get in the car with someone you have just met, especially someone you have met on the Internet. Don't give anyone your address unless you are sure about doing that. Don't go anywhere you wouldn't want your teenage daughter going alone. Make sure you lock the doors after you get in your car. Take simple but sure precautionary measures.

Getting Your Finances in Order

For us, as single women, safety can mean physical safety, but it means financial safety and security, too. That means figuring out our day-to-day financial needs and how to meet them. This means taking stock of insurance, retirement, savings and everything else we need to support ourselves, our children and others dependent on us. It means figuring out how to pay the bills and pay the taxes and keep track of important documents.

Early on, one member of the Radical group discovered that her health insurance premium more than doubled when she was taken off of her husband's group plan. We all discovered complications and problems with health insurance. We found that we were considered higher risk if we had a history of visits to a counselor or therapist. Two of us had our rates go up because we had, for one, an irregular pap smear, and for me, an irregular mammogram that required a breast biopsy. Even though the results were negative in both cases, our insurance premiums went up anyway.

Health insurance has become a huge issue because it is so necessary, yet so expensive for a single woman, especially if you are a single woman without a job. Even employees find that many employers are cutting down on employee benefits including insurance. Ask around. Find out if any organization you belong to provides a special group rate for members. In the end, you may have to bite the bullet and just get the best deal you can find.

Another thing the Radical group discovered was that after our divorce notices were published in the local paper—right below the marriage announcements—almost all of us received calls from people wanting to "take care of our money." Most of the first Radical group had been married to professionals. Most of us had retirement funds. I had never paid much attention to all that. I hardly ever looked at the monthly update on our investments. My husband paid all of the bills, took care of all of the insurance, made all the decisions about investing. When I look back, I realize that was dumb. Very dumb. "What in the world was I thinking" dumb! But my husband was a math major. He was good at that—or I thought he was. I wasn't.

I should have paid more attention, and I'll admit he occasionally tried to get me to. The first time I actually got a grip on our financial situation was after our divorce when I started paying the bills. I hope that most of you have already been paying the bills and know more than I did about the family finances. I have no idea why I turned over that whole job to him. My dad had always been the bill payer when I was growing up, but really, I just didn't have any desire to do it. As I said, that was very dumb.

Don't get me wrong. I appreciated all of the extras of being a professional's wife. We took wonderful vacations. We had a warm, comfortable house where we could spread out and entertain family and friends. Each driver in the family had his or her own car—even though we forced each new driver to drive our old '70s gold station wagon for a while. But we had more trouble than I realized at the time paying our bills. My then-husband had figured out how to juggle things around so that we stayed afloat. We had second mortgages and commercial property that constantly demanded funding for some reason or another.

I take my share of responsibility for our situation, because even though I knew it was precarious, I didn't realize how precarious and demand that we take concrete steps to get our financial life in order. Now that I am on my own, I have no excuse.

One Radical woman's husband slowly, without her knowing, took out all the money her grandparents had left for her children's college educations along with all of the rest of their savings. Her family, when we were growing up together, had been one of the most well-off in our class. After her husband drained those savings, she was left with absolutely nothing, and she never got one bit of financial help from him. She was devastated and sad for a while, but then she figured out she had better just get to work. She did and she has been a tremendous success. It meant long, hard, but satisfying, years of determined effort. She has helped innumerable disadvantaged children and their families by her efforts, and she is proud of what she has accomplished. Another one of the Radical women has started her own business and is putting her unique talents to work. The last I heard, her ex-husband lives in "their" house on the lake and smokes pot with a long line of girlfriends closer to his children's ages than his own.

After our divorce, I wanted to figure out exactly where I stood financially and how to get a solid grip on all of the money issues. Luckily, I was getting alimony and child support. Our counselor said to me, "I have a friend who is president of a local, independent bank not far from you. Go see him and tell him your situation." So I did. I went into his office, sat down and started crying as I was trying to tell him what was going on. He got a box of tissues, put it on the table, and we started talking about the basics.

I opened up a checking and a savings account in my name. He gave me a loan for $25,000, just on my word, to cover an expense that had to be paid before my ex-husband could come up with the money he owed on that expense. The bank president was very kind, helpful and realistic. Find a bank like that, or find someone at a bank who will sit down with you like that. I still do business at that bank. They know me; they know my situation; they

> *"She was devastated and sad for a while, but then she figured out she had better just get to work. She did and she has been a tremendous success".*

know my weaknesses. Plus, with online banking I can now go on the Internet and see exactly how much money I have instead of calling Jane at the front desk and having her look it up! Find a helpful, friendly, personal bank and bank officer. It's wonderful when I drive up to the bank window, and the staff knows my name and asks how things are going.

Now, I actually enjoy paying the bills. I know exactly how much I have. I know exactly how much money I owe. I know approximately what I will have coming in every month, and if I don't have the money, I try to do without. I almost always pay off my credit card bills when they come. I hate paying that interest!

I usually get a cup of coffee or a glass of cider, put on some great music, maybe light a candle and pay the bills. Being in control of that, and making decisions, even the decisions not to spend what I don't have, feels good.

I know some of the women in our Radical Group had little or no financial support from their husbands. Several ex-husbands never paid one cent of alimony or child support. One well-off surgeon continually made things hard for his wife and their college-age children. One woman in our group, who got virtually nothing from her ex-husband, had to move out of her house into a small, depressing apartment for a while.

Things can be very tough financially for many of the women in a midlife divorce. Statistics show that, almost universally, women are worse off financially five years after the divorce, and husbands are almost always better off than when they decided to leave their families. Wherever you find yourself on the money wheel, remember that God promises he will provide what we need if we put him first in our lives. I know that's hard to believe when there are bills to pay and no money to pay them. I don't know how it's worked, but so far, I have always had enough to get through each month.

One good help can be to sign up for one of the national money-management courses offered through churches. Some churches even pay part of the fee. Many people swear by these programs, and are out of debt to prove it!

It's painful to know that some of our husbands have never taken responsibility for their own families after they went off with their new love. It's hard to comprehend that. One father I know of doesn't even know his daughter just delivered a beautiful baby boy. Some of us, of course, have it much tougher than others. But whatever your situation, tackle those big financial issues head on. They won't go away, so the sooner we get control of them the better.

If you are going to use a financial planner, find someone you trust. I found a financial planner who sat down and did a financial profile and helped me figure out exactly where I was with my money. He didn't charge for those visits, and his counsel got me started on the right foot. His help was very reassuring. Be careful with people who get a commission on the products they provide. Ask around. Be curious and cautious. Get ideas from several sources.

What you need is a good understanding of what you have coming in, what you have going out, how to protect yourself from financial disaster, and how to plan for the future. Don't forget, you will have everyone in the world wanting to "take care of your money." You take care of it yourself! The person or company you choose for financial guidance can make a huge difference in how much money you will have for the rest of your life. Make the decision carefully and wisely.

I also consulted with the friend and accountant who had done our taxes every year. He gave me advice about the tax consequences of selling the house, ideas about my home-based business and counsel about lots of other financial issues. He knew my background. He understood my predicament, and he had biked across our state with the same group we had on several occasions. (You can almost always trust someone you have biked across your state with!) He gave me good, sound, practical advice. He also did my tax returns the first few years because I had no idea how to do them. The tax forms used during a divorce are even more complicated than the *normal* crazy array!

At first I put the money from our retirement funds into a simple CD-type account that drew interest like a savings account. I had too many things to deal with to even begin to think about what to do with that lump sum of money. As it turned out, not long after I put the money in that account, stocks started going down, and they continued to go down for a good while. Meanwhile, my money was safely gaining interest—not much, really, but at least I didn't lose any money when lots of other people did.

I later chose a man from our church who was highly recommended to help with my investments. Even though he is probably 15 to 20 years younger than I am, I feel like I'm talking to my Dad when I ask to take money out of that account. He doesn't like for me to do that unless it's an absolute emergency. He helped me put my money in funds with just enough risk and just enough security. Since I have absolutely no experience in investing, I was glad to find someone I could trust to take care of my money for me. I didn't have time, and I didn't want the pressure.

When I was getting my financial self in order, one thing I did was decide to give a tenth of my income to the church. In the beginning that felt like a fairly big chunk of what I had coming in. I made the conscious choice to do with less, to cut down somewhere else. It gave me a feeling of control and power over my own financial decisions. When it's your choice, it seems less like a sacrifice and more like a choice—a conscious decision to help someone else or a worthwhile cause. God specifically commands us to give to the poor and to be generous. You stop wondering, "How am I going to survive?" or "How will I ever pay the bills?" and start focusing on helping someone else and sharing God's amazing generosity. This law proves true no matter how much or how little you have.

Early in the process, I went to my accountant so he could help me with my budget. I showed him the 10 percent giving idea. His one suggestion was that I get my two credit cards paid off before I started on that plan. At that time I owed about $10,000, so I paid off as much as I could every month until those debts and their ridiculous finance charges were gone. I think that was good advice. However, if you are racking up credit card expenses and never getting your balance paid down, I think it would be better to go ahead and give the amount you've committed to God. Then, pay off the credit cards as you go.

God can help you with your debts just like he can help you with everything else. But it takes discipline and determination on your part. Don't put off committing to God, because once you do, you will understand—even if it's hard to verbalize—that he will truly give you everything you need. Try it. We are all abundantly blessed, and we can choose how to spend or not spend our money. I believe God rewards that attitude when we share what he gives us.

I know for me it was scary to start, but once I started giving even that small amount, new jobs started coming my way almost immediately. I don't know whether it was because I simply decided to believe that God would provide as he promised he would, or that I was more confident and less apprehensive about whether I could make my business a success. But it was amazing, really. I know! I know! This kind of talk can get weird and unbelievable, but really, it works.

LISTING YOUR YEARLY GOALS

That next year on January 1, I chose my verse for the year, and I made a list of goals that I wanted to reach. Here is my verse from Jeremiah and my list:

"For I know the plans I have for you," declares the Lord, "plans to prosper you and not to harm you, plans to give you hope and a future. You will come and pray to me, and I will listen to you. You will seek me and find me when you seek me with all your heart."

My Goals:
1. Consciously commit absolutely everything I am and have to God every day.
2. Share God's extravagant love.
3. Pass along God's outrageous generosity.

4. Give 10 percent each month to God as a demonstration of my commitment.
5. Earn enough each month including alimony to reach a good salary figure.
6. Publish "Radical Recovery."
7. Make each client more successful.
8. Create living spaces that are warm, fun and ordered.
9. Be a fit, healthy, strong 125 pounds.
10. Take the whole family on a great vacation.

This was my list. I read it every single morning and every single night. I prayed about every item on that list every day. I purposely put my goal of giving to the church before the goal of making a certain amount each month. I wanted to prove what God said was true. He says if we in faith make a decision to give to him, he will repay us. I don't understand how that works. And I don't think it's just financial blessings. I think it's a mental attitude of plenty, of certainty, of confidence that I will be, not just okay, but sharing in God's extravagant love and outrageous generosity.

It seems that first of all you have to give yourself to God completely. You have to commit not just your money, but your whole life. Your intelligence, your home, your creativity, your problems, your dreams, your days, your nights, every single minute of every single day. When you do that, your whole life changes, finances included.

I think one thing that happens is that once you commit totally to God even on a smaller scale to give a certain amount—and you are faithful to that—God blesses you with more to share. If you have proven yourself willing to share whatever you have, God recognizes and rewards that. In that way, God is working through you to accomplish his purposes. This may sound like a wild-eyed televangelist pleading for you to send him your paycheck, but it absolutely happened in my case. I discovered that my wants changed, and I definitely could buy the things I really needed, and I could be more generous as well. I still have a lot to learn about running a business, but God is definitely providing clients and opportunities to help me do that, and I'm finding joy and personal satisfaction in the process.

I hesitate to even talk about this much, because I know, as I said, that some religious shows say, "Send in your money. If you do, God will send you more and more back," sort of like a cosmic poker game. They seem to bargain with God, "I will give this much so you will give me that much."

I don't agree with that kind of thinking. I don't believe that is what the Bible teaches. I think it does teach, however, that when we give our *worry* about money to God, when we decide to honor him by giving back a part of what he has so richly blessed us with, he frees us up to develop a sharing attitude, an attitude of abundance, an attitude that says, "I am going to spend today enjoying my work and believing God will bless it so that I can share those blessings with others. I'm going to do my absolute best. I am going to seek to enrich other people by my work, and I will leave the results up to God." That attitude brings an amazing freedom and sense of serenity about both our work and our money, and about sharing what God has so generously given us.

I'm proud of my growing financial independence, but I am not going to pretend that I don't have workdays of complete chaos and strife. I still have clients who need things yesterday. I still have to skimp and scrounge occasionally to pay the bills. I still have printing mistakes that must be rectified out of my pocket. I still have difficult situations that I have to work out, but somehow the whole thing is more of a challenge—an adventure—a wonderful opportunity to let God do his work through fallible, unorganized, still-a-lot-to-learn me.

As my mom would say, it's a "standing on tiptoes" way to live, and it changes your attitude about everything. I do have to tell you that there is one thing on my list that I haven't done yet, and that is take the whole family on a great vacation. I'm not giving up on that—I just haven't been able to pull it off so far.

ORGANIZING YOUR PAPERS

After decluttering and getting your financial bearings, you will need to establish one place where you always put important documents and papers. It's helpful to have one file box for that purpose only—a box you can grab easily if your house ever caught on fire! Most home accessories stores or business supply stores or organizing centers have all kinds of file boxes to fit every filing need. Or you could have one drawer in your file cabinet. Regardless where you decide to keep them, you must be able to locate, organize and take care of the documents listed on the opposite page. Make a copy of this list to put with your papers.

Keep all of your important papers in one spot, and make sure someone you trust knows how to locate your papers as well. You may want to keep copies of many of these papers at home, and put the originals in a safety deposit box at your local bank.

Okay, so now you're decluttered, organized and have your papers in order. It's time for the "Radical Woman Lifesavers"—essential and helpful hints that will make your life much, much easier!

The Radical Lifesavers:

• Keep a Master Planner—it will be your extra brain!

Get a great daily planner with features you like, and use it! When you are going through a divorce, your brain is under terrible stress. It needs all the help it can get.

All my adult life I have used little 8 1/2" x 5 1/2" daily planners, which fit great in my purse. When I was first struggling with my husband's affair and all the following upheaval, I could hardly remember my phone number. During that time, my counselor suggested I get a big, 8 1/2" x 11" planning book with two full pages for each day. One page has a task list and time slots to fill in, the other is for whatever information I want to remember. I write poetry, make notes of memorable thoughts, and include all kinds of reminders.

IMPORTANT DOCUMENT
Checklist

Important documents
- ☐ Wills
- ☐ Divorce documents
- ☐ Birth certificates
- ☐ Passport

Financial Records
- ☐ Tax returns
- ☐ Receipts and expense documentation
- ☐ Investment documents
- ☐ Alimony documents and receipts
- ☐ Child support documents and receipts

Insurance certificates
- ☐ Health
- ☐ Auto
- ☐ Life
- ☐ Home
- ☐ Disability
- ☐ Long-term care

House Information
- ☐ Titles
- ☐ Mortgage documents and records
- ☐ Home improvement records

Car Information
- ☐ Titles
- ☐ Payments
- ☐ Service records

Bank and Investment Records

- ☐ Make a new three-ring binder notebook every year to keep:
  Monthly bank statements and information
  Monthly investment summaries and records.

My planner has room for lots of great information, and I fill it up. Keeping the following information readily at hand will make your life so much easier! Be sure your planner has a spot for all this:

- Monthly budget sheets and yearly income tracking sheets
- Automobile servicing information and records
- Identification numbers
- Password information
- Medical information
- Employment information
- Clothing sizes
- Friend and family information
- Medical emergency numbers
- Family medical information
- Physical statistics records
- A list of birthdays and anniversaries

Some people don't like to keep all of that vital information in one spot, but I have never lost my book for any significant length of time, and I am prone to losing things. At some point I will go back to a smaller book, but during this upheaval it's good to have a central place for my vital papers and documents, *and* a book I can take with me that serves as my brain backup!

• Keep a Little List.

Keep a list or file of business cards or newspaper ads for good, reliable, inexpensive workers and professionals, so you are prepared if you need one of these:

- Attorney
- Automobile mechanic/service department
- Dentist
- Electrician
- Financial advisor
- Handyman

- Internist
- Gynecologist
- Plumber
- Specialist

• Take Care of Your Car and House.

My dad took care of a battalion of tanks in WW II, and he knows that regular maintenance is the best policy for lots of reasons. Preventive check-ups and service for your body, your car and your house are investments in the future, and will ward off serious problems down the line.

Change the oil in your car when you are supposed to and get your periodic services done on schedule. Even though recommended service is expensive and is easy to let slide, in the long run it pays such great dividends.

As for your house, I know of an older woman who had been widowed for many years yet kept her house in excellent condition. She was a teacher, and every summer she undertook a significant repair or improvement on her home. Her house was a pleasure to be in, and she drew comfort and serenity from her up-to-date surroundings.

• Work out a Chore Calendar.

Life is complicated, and when you are going through a divorce it is chaos. Getting a good handle on various important chores and when during the year they need doing will give you so much peace of mind. I try to schedule different appointments or tasks near memorable dates or milestones.

Below is a list of necessary tasks and suggestions about when to do them. Work out your own list.

- Schedule *a pap smear and mammogram* near your birthday.
- Have your *teeth cleaned* every six months. Pick a month that triggers your memory.
- Have the *air conditioner checked* out every other year in the spring.
- Have the *furnace checked* out every other year in the fall. These maintenance checks will pay dividends with lower utility bills.

- Change *the filter on the furnace* every other month. Mark the days on your calendar. Ask the technician to show you how.
- Change the *smoke alarm batteries* at Thanksgiving.
- Clean *leaves and debris* away from the outside air conditioning unit every spring.
- Have the *gutters cleaned* every spring, as well. Hire someone to do this if you need to. Gutters full of leaves and debris cause roof leaks and other problems.

Being organized gives you some sense of control in your life. Depression occurs most often in people who have no sense of control over their circumstances, and as you know, there are many things in this situation that you have absolutely no power over. But you can maintain control over some things. You can get your home and work environments uncluttered and functional.

One of my goals was to have my home environment "warm, fun and ordered." It's comforting and reassuring when that's how your home feels. It's calming when you have your important papers in order. It's empowering when you know your true financial situation, and you begin to take positive, definite steps to deal with it. When you have a plan for taking care of your health, your home and your car, you feel more secure. All of these steps give you authority over important parts of your life.

You can't control what your ex-husband did or still does, but you can decide how you will deal with your own day-to-day obligations and responsibilities. Begin right now to set your sights to get from where you are to where you want to be financially. You have your own special abilities, and you have the all-powerful God of the universe living inside you. He will continually bless you with everything good.

CHAPTER FOUR

HELP YOUR CHILDREN

*As hard as this divorce is
on you, it's even harder
on your children.
Know what they need more
than anything else?
For you to be yourself,
and be okay.*

Those words from a song from the '70s express in a nutshell the main reason we need to stay connected to people who have our best interests at heart. When we're weak, they encourage us and build us up. They "give us hope to carry on," and now, especially, we need that. Someday, maybe soon, we can help carry someone else.

Everywhere we turn in literature, in music, in the Bible or deep in our own hearts, we are reminded that we need each other. We need each other in the good times, and so much more so when catastrophe hits. Here's what King Solomon said centuries ago in the book of Ecclesiastes: "Two are better than one ... If one falls down, his friend can help him up. But pity the man who falls and has no one to help him up."

Get Together

"Sometimes in our lives
We all have pain
We all have sorrow
But if we are wise
We know that there's
always tomorrow
Lean on me, when
you're not strong
And I'll be your friend
I'll help you carry on
For it won't be long
'Til I'm gonna need
Somebody to lean on"

Right now, you probably feel more disconnected than you have been in your whole life. The simple ugly fact is that a midlife divorce destroys relationships. Besides destroying the original relationship of husband and wife, it changes all of the relationships surrounding that central connection. It also dismantles an irreplaceable part of who we are—a member of an intact primary family. The dissolution of our original family alters relationships with our children, our extended families, our social groups, our neighborhoods and even our church. Most seriously, it alters how we think about ourselves. Virtually all of our social connections are at risk, and we often feel helpless to do anything about it.

Literally everyone in our circle of connections is influenced by our divorce. For us as midlife ex-wives, the biggest problem is that often our social networks were built around our husband's career and our children's activities, both of which are probably gone at this point. In my case, all but one of our children were in college or married. Toward the end of my divorce, those activities that revolved around my one son still at home dissolved when he left for a college that felt halfway around the world.

All of these changed relationships are incredibly hard to deal with, especially early on. In my mind, everyone knew that my charming, good-looking, successful husband decided I was not worth his faithfulness, and that his girlfriend was more fun, sexier and more interesting than I. Everywhere I went, I felt awkward and alone. Suddenly, I was having to go places not just alone, but from my point of view as a rejected, discarded, irrelevant woman. To me the whole situation was a heart-rending private and excruciatingly public humiliation.

The question is: *What can we do about it?* How can we get through this ordeal with less pain? How can we face this part of our life in a better way? Can we hurry this process along? Is there any possible way to grow from these sad, lonely, seemingly devastating feelings of insecurity, distress and loss? The Radical Women tried to find practical, realistic answers to all of these difficult questions.

OUR CHILDREN — OUR GREATEST CONCERN

Even though we were all trying to maintain personal balance, the issue we most worried about was how to help our children. For every woman around the table at our first Radical meetings, the biggest concern was maintaining and strengthening our own connections with our children, and our biggest worry was how all the losses were really affecting them. We cried about it. Most of us privately begged God to help us know how to help our children. We talked with our counselors about it.

For our children, their father's midlife breakdown and our divorce were life-changing, disconcerting, uncomfortable realities that they were caught in the middle of and had absolutely no control over. That truth usually made us mad at our ex-husbands all over again, and of course, sad about all that had been lost.

Some of our children did better than others. One of the Radical Women's daughters is a wonderful, fun, darling girl who was in junior high and high school when her father "fell in love" with "Alexandra." In fact, her father left their family to be with her. At one point this Radical daughter refused to attend extended family functions because, she said, "We're not a real family anymore. I feel like I'm on the outside looking in at this great family, and I'm not really a part of that family anymore because our family is gone." She lost interest in school. She quit the track team. For a while she emotionally dropped out of about everything to some extent.

Another woman's son refused to see, talk to or have anything to do with his father, and still doesn't to this day. What a huge hurt in that young man's life. His father had an affair with an administrative assistant from his office who "really understood him" and married her. Children all react differently, but on the inside they are all—just as we are—trying desperately to adjust to this new unexpected reality the best they can.

We may not know the real effect of this situation on our children until they begin making relationship commitments of their own. I often prayed that God would use this to help make their marriages stronger, that they would see what devastation affairs have on a relationship, and that they would realize how important it is to face problems in a marriage before they get to the point where they can't be fixed.

All of the Radical children who were welcomed as tiny babies, toddlers, preteens, teens, and young adults are suddenly faced, not with the warm, loving family they had always known, but with the ugly destruction of that core entity. For most of their lives, my children had wonderful security as part of a happy intact family with a happily married father and mother. They knew we had things to work through like every other family, but they also knew we put our bond as a family above all those disagreements and disturbances.

One Radical son wrote on his college application that he came from that rare but solid background of a happy, intact family with a Dad who went to work every morning and a Mom who stayed home and took care of things on that front. A Radical daughter, after a weekend of bonding with her sorority sisters her second year in college, had said she was one of the few girls in the house whose parents weren't divorced, and how proud she was of having an intact family. That suddenly was gone. A strong family was important to the children of all the Radical Women in our group no matter what their ages.

Unlike many of our children's friends, whose parents had given up long ago, and who were now part of blended families, stepfamilies or single-parent homes, our children experienced a solid, stable, good home for most of their lives. One of the Radical sons said that it still bothered him when friends said to him, "Well, at least you were older when it happened." Even though our children are older and better able to figure out what's going on, the divorce of your parents is no easier to accept. The divorce is often harder to understand and come to grips with because often it is completely unexpected. It catches almost all of us, especially our children, off guard.

A midlife affair and the ensuing divorce bring peripheral problems for grown children in their own relationships. The married or engaged sons of Radical Women were trying hard to convince their wives or fiancées that they would never do this kind of thing. The girls were saying, "You had *better* not ever do this!" One future daughter-in-law said to her fiancé, "I will not be as patient as your mom has been. One time with another woman and you are gone. You will not get any second chances."

Two of my children got married during this ordeal. I wondered if our children thought, when planning or saying wedding vows, that those same vows didn't actually mean that much to their father. Maybe they didn't think that at all, but I have to admit, I thought about it, and it made me unbelievably sad.

WHAT THE FATHERS LOSE

As devastating as the cold, hard facts of our husbands' affairs are on us as wives, I think they are often even more disorienting to our children. In fact, I could understand my husband wanting to leave me for someone younger or more accomplished or more beautiful, but I absolutely could not understand how he could leave our children or the family we had built. Of course, our husbands say they are not leaving their children, but the fact is they are giving up the normal everyday contact that happens in an intact, primary family. I could not understand how my husband could tell our children by his actions, "nurturing and protecting this family is not as important to me as my new-found happiness."

Our husbands also all told their children in one way or another, "This is not about you. This has nothing to do with you" when in reality it has everything to do with them. Their father's decision destroys something they cherished. His affair destroys something they found strength and comfort in. His actions forever change a family that they took pride in for all those years. One night when I was crying about the fact that our family "was destroyed," our middle son said to me, "No, our family is not destroyed. In fact, in some ways it is stronger than ever. It's just that Dad has decided not to be a part of it. We are still a family." Even though what he said is true, their father's long-term affair and the end of our marriage changes life for our children and grandchildren on so many levels forever.

Nevertheless, our ex-husbands continue to act as if this change in life has nothing to do with their children. In most of the Radical families, the husbands are willing to give up sitting together as a primary family at their children's marriages. They are willing to give up going to the hospital together to welcome new grandchildren. They are willing to give up taking care of grandchildren together. In fact, they are willing to give up *all* of those things that intact families do. Even though I still do not understand how giving up all that is possible, the sad fact is that it's not just possible, it's a reality. Our husbands have decided they are willing to be with another family most of the time, and that this new family will be just as good—or maybe better—than his old family, except maybe on weekends or on trips or something.

Our husbands also think their girlfriends should be embraced with open arms by their children and grandchildren. One daughter said to her dad, "I don't want to meet your girlfriend. I don't want her in my house. I don't want to ever see her face. If you marry her, I will have to figure out how to deal with that, but right now, I don't want to have anything to do with her. If my best friend did this, I wouldn't support her either." Her father thought she was being unfairly hard on him. When he asked her, "What am I supposed to do," she replied disgustedly, "You figure it out."

Our ex-husbands tell our children by their actions that keeping promises is not really that important. They are saying in a sense, "do whatever makes you feel good." Our divorce means that every single holiday, every single celebration, every single family occasion will be complicated, and in my perception at the beginning, tarnished. Trying to coordinate family gatherings is complicated enough after your children marry. Now it's unbelievably more complex, and our children and grandchildren are the ones who have to make most of the adjustments.

Remember to assure your children that you understand their predicament and verbalize to them that you want them to do what is best for their families and not to feel the pressure of trying to please everyone all of the time. That's impossible in the best of situations, and even more so now. Your children will appreciate that attitude on your part because they are struggling to make all of these adjustments, too.

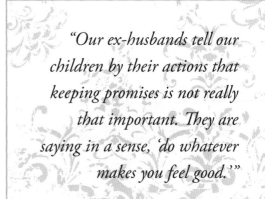

"Our ex-husbands tell our children by their actions that keeping promises is not really that important. They are saying in a sense, 'do whatever makes you feel good.'"

My problem in the beginning was that I felt that this situation was my ex-husband's doing, and he should be the one to make the adjustments in his life. That doesn't usually happen, and, of course, he's putting pressure on the children from his side of the situation. The last thing our children need is more pressure from us.

A midlife crisis father, whether he realizes it or not, changes his children's deepest, gut-level feelings about him forever. For some reason, that's not important enough at the time to make him change his direction. One divorced and remarried dad actually said to his son during a confrontation at a graduation ceremony, "Get over it—people get divorced all the time. It's not the end of the world." So much for being sensitive and trying to teach the right life lessons. But to that dad, and many of the other dads, the repercussions of their life decisions seemed to be really no big deal. Their new-found happiness seems to be their biggest concern.

One of the things that Radical Women have to deal with is that many men compensate for their guilt by trying to prove to everyone what good guys they really are, and they suddenly become Super Dads. They woo their children with stuff, trips, fun and visits. It's the old story: "we do the discipline, while they do Disneyland"—along with probably *doing* Debbie or Trixie as well.

Others are so obsessed with their new love that they have little time for their own children. Some drop out of the picture forever with hardly a word. In one family the father was a leader in a church, and he left for another state with a married woman from the same congregation. He has little communication with his children. He and his new wife have toddler twins about the same age as a grandchild he has never seen.

As much as these men try to pretend otherwise, affairs, selfishness and divorce have *everything* to do with their children and the whole extended family. Even though most dads say to their children in some way or another, "This situation is between your mom and me and has nothing to do with you," in reality each dad has tarnished something deeply important to his children: his long-term commitment to their mother, to their primary family, and ultimately to them and their own children. They will never think of him in quite the same way, no matter what he does. That loss of respect is simply one of the lasting consequences of the choices he has made.

Knowing all of that, we as mothers, grandmothers and friends must be careful not to do ugly, hateful things that will cause people to lose respect for us, too. We need to display decent and honorable actions through all of this, as hard as it is.

I know it's difficult, especially at the beginning, to even speak in a civil tone of voice most of the time. Even though we often have thoughts of revenge and retaliation, we need to realize that those kinds of thoughts don't hurt our ex-spouses or their girlfriends. All they do is hurt us and prolong our healing process. Remember, too, that thoughts can lead to actions, and the things we're thinking could easily result in actions that could put us in jail for the rest of our lives!

At one of the Radical meetings, one of the women said that her counselor told her, "Your children will only deal with this as well as you do." All of us looked at each other in desperation. One put her head on the table and said, "Please! Please don't tell me that. I'm falling apart. I'm not doing well with this at all." We all felt like that. Now, not only do we have to deal with our own despair, but we are also told we are responsible for how our children come through this! I remember thinking, "This is my husband's doing. It's not mine. I didn't want this. He's the one sleeping with someone else. Now you're telling me I'm responsible if my children don't do well through this?"

As much as we hate to admit it, the counselor was right. Some of the Radical Women felt that was an unfair burden to put on us, and that we don't have to take responsibility for the affects of this situation on our children. I agree that we don't have to take responsibility for our husbands' choices, but we do have to conduct ourselves now in a way that will help our children and not harm them further. Our children are looking to us for direction, for strength, for security. Most of our husbands, their fathers, are completely off in midlife crisis la-la land. We are the most sane part of the picture, and I admit that is really scary. The trouble is, right when our children need us the most, we are often at our worst.

AVOIDING WHAT YOU'LL REGRET

My children have seen me do ridiculous things. My children have seen me enraged like never before. I didn't plan for them to see it, but they were often in range when something happened that sent either me or their father almost off the deep end. I pray that God will protect them from the harmful long-term effects of those things.

One father, a well-known, respected member of the community, on one weekend morning grabbed a knife and ran to the garage as if he was going to do something terribly harmful. The distraught wife called her son to her side and opened the garage door hoping that seeing his son would prevent any irrational behavior. I only tell that story to remind you that all of us can lose sight of reality through this, and emotions on both sides can be violent and unpredictable. Try to remember that all of these actions and how you deal with them are affecting your children—positively or negatively.

I am going to tell you a couple of experiences of mine that I hate to admit. I'm telling you because I want you to realize that all of us as Radical Women have done ridiculous, out of character, embarrassing things through this ordeal. You probably will, too. Just remember to think about how your actions are affecting your children. Most of the time emotions and situations are thrust upon us before we have time to think at all, so we react emotionally and at a gut level.

Right now, stop reading long enough to plan how you will react to emotion-charged situations that have the power to make you berserk. Write your plans down on the opposite page. My ex-husband had a few specific phrases that sent me into the upper stratosphere of anger, so my counselor helped me figure out and practice saying appropriate responses in a calm, careful voice. You know what your own buttons are, so be ready for them. Practice your responses if you need to. If you've already acted in a way you regret, take responsibility for those actions, apologize for them, ask for forgiveness—then move on. That's all you can do. In our case, I did several things that I am now absolutely mortified and ashamed about.

Plan Ahead &
AVOID WHAT YOU'LL REGRET:

What triggers—phrases, circumstances, situations—
make me act crazy?

_____

_____

_____

_____

_____

_____

_____

_____

_____

To avoid acting crazy and in ways I'll regret, the next time
those triggers occur, I will:

_____

_____

_____

_____

_____

_____

_____

_____

_____

_____

For all of our married life, I had hoped that my husband and I could share a spiritual bond. That never really happened. I tried to make it clear before we got married that I wanted our home to be fun, intellectually lively and centered on God. For some reason, a real spiritual closeness never developed. One devastating day after more than two years of my husband's continuing affair, I found out that my husband had turned our van into a convenient love nest for him and his girlfriend the night before. I told him *he* could either tell me about it, or I would take what I found in the back seat to the authorities, and they could tell me about it.

He told me about it, so I told him to leave the house, and that I was going to file for divorce. The next day he called and said he was going to start going to men's Bible study. I'm embarrassed to say that his call made me sad and enraged at the same time. A deeper spiritual connection was one of the things I wanted most for us to share. Now after the "back of the van" incident, that's when he decided suddenly to be more spiritual.

I thought, "I've wanted this for years. Now, when he has made it impossible for us to live together, he's going to get religion." All those years I wanted to share a spiritual bond, and now not only had he found the light of his life in this other woman, but he was going to "find God," too. And I was going to miss it all. I was furious at him, and even worse, I was furious at God!

One morning not long after this incident, he stopped by our house and was standing in the back entry when something was said about his Bible study. I absolutely fell apart when he started talking about the class. I had a long roll of gift-wrapping paper in my hand, and I started swinging it around trying to hit him and the wall and the door and whatever else I could. For the first time in my life I think, I was absolutely, completely, totally out of control. I may have grown temporary fangs and been frothing at the mouth. I don't know, and at the time, I didn't care. In looking back, if I had had a hammer in my hand or a butcher knife, he might be dead and I might be in prison.

That day my faith in God was at its lowest point. I was devastated and furious that God was going to let my husband destroy our family, and not only that, but that my husband was suddenly going to find God, with this other woman as his partner. I was furious at God. I was furious at my husband—and all because he said he was going to Bible study. How is that for having a Christian attitude? A stronger spiritual connection was something I had prayed for. Now God was giving it to my husband with this other woman, and I was acting like a crazy person.

Our children said, "He's doing this because he knows this is the only thing that will make you take him back." A friend of ours said, "If he really does find God, he will understand that what he is doing by continuing this affair is absolutely wrong, and he will come back to make things right with you. If he doesn't come to that conclusion, you can rest assured this Bible study is nothing more than something to make himself look and feel better."

My ex-husband would probably deny this, but he seemed to make a point of dropping into the conversation as often as he could that he was going to Bible Study on Monday nights. He usually didn't tell anyone what he was doing with another man's wife later in the week. How can people think badly of him when he goes to a Bible study and plays the piano for their meetings as well? I was sick at heart about the whole thing.

Our youngest son heard my out-of-control behavior that morning. He just quietly left by another door and walked down the street to a friend's house. How heartbreaking is that? How humiliating! And then we're told our children are only going to do as well as we are doing? We were all absolutely terrified by that thought.

Another horribly embarrassing day also had to do in a way with something religious. At the time this next event happened, my husband was supposedly not seeing this woman any more. He was writing me cards and letters promising his faithfulness. He was calling on the phone, pleading for me to let him prove once and for all his trustworthiness. Well, on one Sunday morning, our youngest son and I were on our way to worship services. In our family, the rule was that Sunday morning church attendance was mandatory as long as children were living at home. Once off to college they could make their own decision about it, even though I tried my best, and still try with our youngest, to admonish them from afar!

Anyway, on our way to church we had to drive by the street where my husband's apartment was. I saw my husband's girlfriend biking away from his apartment onto the street where we were driving. I drove the car beside her as close as I could get and yelled out the window, "I'm so glad you've taken up biking!" If my son hadn't been in the car, I'm sure I would have yelled something much worse. Anyway, driving slow enough to yell at someone on a bike is hard, so I yelled that and went up to the corner and turned around so I could drive past her again, and I said something about her "dorky" bicycling outfit or some other equally ridiculous comment.

She turned around and went back toward the apartments, so I turned around and drove past her again. It was pathetic, and even more so considering the fact that our son was in the car with me, and we were on our way to church. I think he finally said, "Mom, let's go."

I still hang my head in disbelief and shame that I had so little control at that moment. I hate that my son saw me like that. All I can say is, "I'm sorry." However, I'll admit that I definitely can understand crimes of passion, because it would not have taken much at that moment for me to run the girlfriend over with my car. I'm glad I'm not in jail for vehicular manslaughter, but I'm still sorry I was so out of control. I pray that my son—and my other children—will forgive me, and that all of those terrible occasions have not damaged them in ways that can't be repaired.

My children, I think, have forgiven me for my sometimes ridiculous behavior. They have all been incredibly supportive. In looking back, I think they helped me through this as much as I helped them, maybe more. I prayed daily in the beginning that God would somehow make them stronger through all of this, and I believe he is continually answering my prayer.

A Brother's Letter About My Children

Sis ...

You've got to display your faith in God by living it out in your life. Your kids will give you some time and space. They will be gentle with you for a while. They will encourage you and comfort you and support you as best they can. But eventually, your kids aren't going to want to be around you if you're sad or angry all the time. They don't want to deal with your disappointment, your despair, your broken dreams, your melancholy memories forever. They're busy trying to get on with things themselves, and it will encourage them to see you take life by the throat and live it boldly, joyfully, confidently....

Stop worrying. Stop worrying about the kids so much. Ask God to protect and comfort and empower them. You can't change what's happened in their lives, but you can help them become stronger people. Stop worrying that they will start thinking your wayward partner is okay, and that you caused all of this. Stop worrying that they will suddenly accept and embrace him and think, "I can understand why Dad needed to get out." Stop worrying that because they spend time with him, they approve of him or see him as a person they want to be like. They see him for what he is. They know what he has done. They know what his character is like. They know those things. They may not say it, but deep down, they know it. They will make their own decisions about him.

Be confident enough in yourself and God to let your kids and everyone else figure out their own lives and relationships to him, and then be content. You just make sure you're being the kind of person you should be. Make sure you're being the kind of person who they can admire and look up to. They can't do that if you're being hateful, angry, or constantly consumed with worry and sadness.

Sis, let your children, your family and your friends see your bright light of faith. It's what they need. It's what you need. It's what the whole world needs. And it will bring you absolutely everything to make your life just like it should be, even now.

I love you,
Your brother, W

What Our Children Told Us

With all of that said and with the acceptance of all of the anger and agony that this kind of situation initially produces, we have to figure out not only how to get emotional and physical control of ourselves, but we have to make our children's way through this as easy as possible. As Radical Women, we decided to ask our children directly what they specifically needed from us during this ordeal.

These are the quotes from the children of our first Radical Group in answer to these questions:

"How can I help you most right now?"

"What do you need from me?"

"Do you have any suggestions that would make things better for you?"

Here are some of their answers. They range from early high school age to their early 30s.

"I need for you to stay true to who you are and be the person you've always been for me."

"I need for you to just be yourself and act the same as always."

"My relationship with you hasn't changed, but if you start changing and acting out of character and weird, then I have two new relationships I have to figure out—the one with Dad and the one with you. I need for you to be like you've always been."

"I just want you to act like nothing's happened. Just remember, you are still the same person. It's Dad who's changed."

"Sometimes I feel like I'm dealing with two adolescents. He's lying and running around. You're crying and following him around doing ridiculous things. You're both acting ridiculous! Just stop it!"

"We are just as much a family as ever—maybe even closer in some ways. Now we're just trying to figure out what to do with this person on the outskirts of our relationships. He can't even seem to figure himself out, so how can we really figure out what we want our relationship to be with him until he at least does that?"

"You have had to figure out how to deal with a person you cannot trust, cannot depend on, who keeps breaking all of his promises. It takes a long time to figure out how to respond to that. That's where I am now. I'm trying to figure out how to deal with Dad who has disappointed us, lied to us, and is now trying to act like it's no big deal. You can't do much about that process. If you try to interfere, it won't work, and it might make us question your motives. Just try to let us figure out our own relationship to him."

"If you don't divorce him, I'm going to run away."

"Stop being so upset about it. I'm sorry you're sad, but just get over it. He's not going to change, so just get over it. It will be easier on all of us."

"I know what happened. I know what Dad did. I'm intelligent enough to figure this out for myself. You don't need to tell me how to feel about Dad."

"I hesitate to do much at all with him because then he and others might think I approve of what he's doing. I'm still trying to figure out how to handle that."

"I don't want either of you to talk about the other. It's hard to know what to believe."

"The thing I hate most is how sad you are. I can hardly stand to see you crying. Sometimes I want to go live somewhere else just so I don't have to see you cry."

"The easiest analogy is this: My Dad as I knew him has passed away. Now, there's this new person I have to figure out what to do with."

"I don't care if I ever see him again. So you don't have to do anything different. Just be yourself and forget about him. He's not worth it."

"If you were widowed, I would want you to get on with life—be enthusiastic, be interested, be involved, be happy, be engaged in life. That's still what I want and need for you to be."

"I am learning to turn off my emotions, so I don't have to think about how sad or mad you are. At school when I start being upset about the situation, I immediately start talking to someone or doing something so I won't have to think about it. I feel like I'm being desensitized to my emotions."

"When I bring our kids to your house, I just want there to be toys in their toy drawer and all the good feelings and special things for them that have always been there."

"Dad was never that emotionally involved anyway. I've tried to talk to him. I just need to accept the fact that my relationship with him will always be pretty superficial, and there's really nothing you can do about that."

"I just want you to be happy you are out of that relationship. Why would you want to stay in any kind of relationship with someone who lies to you, sleeps with another woman and thinks only of himself? Tell me one reason why you would want to have anything to do with a man like that. I want you to be happy, not sad."

"I feel sorry for him. I don't think he will ever really be happy. He's pathetic. His girlfriend is two years older than I am—how pathetic is that? What is wrong with him? I need for you to understand how sick that is, and quit blaming yourself."

"Mom, just live your life. Be happy. She will never take your place. She couldn't. Their relationship will never be anything good because it is all built on lies. He lied to you, to her, to us. She lied to her husband. How could a relationship like that ever be anything good? Just forget him. "

"Just be happy for them. They are perfect for each other. They are both a couple of _ _ _ who are perfect for each other. Just be thankful you are not with him anymore."

"Why are you acting like this—like it's the end of the world? Don't you ever think that God might have something better planned for you?"

"If your religion makes you stay in an abusive relationship like this, I don't want any part of it. Stand up for yourself. Quit taking him back. It's embarrassing."

"The hardest part is the constant arguing."

"Don't try to make me think a certain way about Dad. I know what I think about him. I can come to my own conclusions about what he's doing. You've taught me about right and wrong, so you don't have to try to influence that. I can come to that conclusion myself."

"Even though you tell me you're over it, I know you're not, because you still care what he's doing. Just get over it."

From this list of responses, it's clear that our children, like us, have a lot of figuring out to do.

Many of their responses were, "I've got to figure out how to deal with this," or "I'm trying to figure out ...." We needed to give them space to do that. They are struggling to figure out their dad. We shouldn't be someone they have to figure out as well. They need to know that, while we want what's best for them, they must work out their own relationship with their dad. They need to have the freedom to do that—without worrying about how their decisions will affect us.

> *"Our children need to know that we will be okay—regardless of what they decide about their relationship with their father."*

Our children need to know that we will be okay—regardless of what they decide about their relationship with their father. Their journey is difficult enough under the best of circumstances, and it's even harder if they must constantly worry about how we'll react. Our children don't want a bitter, angry, despairing mother. That's not the mother they know. That's not the mother they need me to be. They need for us to get on with life in a way consistent with who we have always been. I know that's easier said than done, but our children need us to maintain a strong sense of who we are and a strong sense that we will do what's right and what is best for them—just like we have always tried to do.

Let's face it, the person we were married to, our children's father, became someone we didn't know. He became a different person from the man we gave our heart to for all of those years. Our children are struggling to process all of that and what it means in their lives. Be the same caring, fun, concerned mother you've always been, and remember, you're the parent. Your children need to depend on you, not the other way around. My counselor said to me: "You've got one partner in the marriage going completely off the deep end. Your children need one adult in this relationship. They need one stabilizing individual, and it certainly is not going to be your husband. It's going to have to be you, whether you're ready for that or not."

We need, too, to be the same mothers who are not afraid to discipline our children. We are all at such loose ends during this ordeal, and some things can fade into the background. Discipline takes energy and thoughtful consistency, neither of which we have in abundance right now. But discipline is one of those things that needs to be maintained. Our youngest child was in junior high and high school during this upheaval, and I wanted to give him extra leeway because I thought he was going through enough trauma. But children, especially adolescents, want the security of discipline, whether they admit it or not. And they won't admit it. They need to be reassured that the rules of good behavior still apply, despite what their father is doing.

We have a chance to teach our children one of the most important life lessons they will ever learn—that we can't control life. Bad things happen that we don't want. Life presents challenges and difficulties that we have to face. We can grow with those challenges or we can become complainers, whiners and be defeated. As my wonderful sister-in-law said, "We can either be thermostats or thermometers." We each choose how we will respond to life. That lesson of personal responsibility will be invaluable for our children.

It doesn't hurt our children to know how devastated we were about this—how sad—how much we wanted it to be different—how much we struggled to make it right. But when all hope of repair was gone, and I had despaired the loss of the family I had in my dreams, they needed to see me getting back to normal. They eventually needed to see me getting back on my feet, for them, but also for me. They're watching carefully to see how I react to all of this. It will make a difference in how they react to life's challenges in their own future. They are also watching carefully to see how this "trust God" philosophy I have always talked about is playing out in real life. That's very scary and sobering.

In Proverbs, Solomon says, "God-loyal people, living honest lives, make it much easier for their children." Let's be bold enough to trust that truth and live by it. Ask yourself, as one of my brothers encouraged me to do, "What do I want my ultimate spiritual statement to my children to be through all of this?" By keeping in mind your main goal of helping your children in the long run, the daily decisions and actions are easier to manage.

Let your children be involved in decisions that are made. Let them have as much control as possible. When they reach a certain age, they can make their own decisions about which parent they will live with when. Our county gives out a guidebook in every divorce proceeding when children are involved. It shows that older children should have more control. Try not to put any additional pressure on them to spend more time with you, but don't force them to go to Dad's unless specified by the court.

You may decide to tell your child's coaches, teachers or school counselors about the situation at home. The Radical Women had different views about this, but most of us decided to relay the information to a chosen few. Since our son was deeply involved in track, swimming and cross-country in high school, his coaches were invaluable helps. Our son became the 6A Cross-Country champion of Kansas, the two-mile champion and the silver medalist at State in the mile. He also was on the state swim team. Both of his coaches are men of strong character and integrity, and they seem to love both coaching and teaching. I was very grateful for their influence during this time of our son's life.

Even though our son at home kept telling me he was doing fine with all of this, I read a lot about kids not doing so fine—and about kids not wanting to worry their mothers by telling them they weren't fine. Even though our son's grades never faltered, and he continued to be involved in all aspects of school life, I still worried that he was just holding everything in. So, when he was still in junior high school, I made an appointment with the counselor so our son could talk to him privately about anything that he didn't want to talk to me or his dad about—just to be sure.

This is a hard, disruptive, unbelievably challenging situation for you, but let your children see your sense of humor on occasion. Laugh together as often as you can. You can cry later in bed if you need to. Our youngest son and I found things to laugh about several times through this whole ordeal. One time at a swim meet at the high school, when I was already there, his dad came in and, soon after, his dad's girlfriend. I looked across the pool at my son who was sitting with some friends. He kind of shrugged his shoulders and raised his eyebrows as if to say, "What's she doing here?"

That night at home I confided in him that when she walked by, I was really tempted to stand up and push her in the pool, clothes and all. He said, "I wish you would have … my friends and I would have all cheered." That image still flashes through my mind occasionally. It would have been foolish and immature, but I wanted to do it anyway, and I think more than a few people would have been cheering.

At any rate, how our children see us in these circumstances will help them formulate how they will behave when they face hard, unfair, seemingly devastating life circumstances. Make sure the spiritual lessons you are teaching are strong and clear.

Each of my children and their spouses encouraged me in ways that I can't ever thank them enough for. They sent me notes and cards. They called me on the phone. They played the piano for me. My daughter pampered me for a long weekend at her home in Minnesota. They have forgiven me for ridiculous things I have done. And the grandchildren were a comforting delight without even realizing it. In-laws were supportive and helpful as well. I was so blessed, and I feel as though we have all grown together through these hard times.

CHAPTER FIVE

STAY CLOSE TO FAMILY AND FRIENDS

Being self-sufficient is over-rated.
Find someone you can call at 3
in the morning who you know
will pick up the phone.

Although our children are our most pressing concern, we also have to figure out how to deal with all of the extended family relationships. Extended families feel the far-reaching consequences of a broken marriage. Our children's grandparents are affected. Aunts and uncles, nieces, nephews, cousins, and every other member of the extended family have to readjust. My ex-husband's mother still calls me, and as often as not, she cries. My ex-husband's brother and his wife and their children still keep in contact with me and have given me unbelievable support, but because of logistics and our busy lives, I know things will never be exactly the same. We don't connect as often.

In the Radical group, each family situation was different. Some husbands' families shunned the Radical Women in response to what our husbands had said. I have maintained a great relationship with my husband's family even though I think he tried to make it seem as if I was the one unwilling to work things out in our marriage—that I was the one who had ended it. He didn't tell most people that I filed for divorce because he refused to end the relationship with his girlfriend. That was his choice, not mine.

Some of the Radical Women had to deal not only with hostile feelings from their spouse's families, but also with a complete shutdown of contact whatsoever. Divorce is hard on everyone, and families tend to rally around their own. Consequently, their own side of the story is usually the only side they hear. My husband's mother and I had been close, and she knew some of what was really going on. She has always been very supportive to me, and I know without a doubt she wants the best for me and wants me to be happy. However, she said, "Even with what he's done, I will always love [my son] and always support him." I would say the same thing about my sons. But she still feels sad about our divorce. She is still sad that he made the choices he did that resulted in the end of our marriage. She was afraid, at the beginning, that our divorce would change her relationships with her grandchildren.

I was blessed to be born into a very supportive, close-knit family. That central core has been an incredible encouragement to me and to our children. I can speak freely with my parents knowing they will share with me the solid benefits of their wisdom and life-tested experience. I can call either of my brothers at any time during the day or the night about anything and be assured of a heartening, sympathetic ear and both spiritual and practical advice. My sisters-in-law have been encouraging every step of the way, and even my nieces and nephews have done everything they could to make me feel better. I have been very blessed.

My extended family has continued our yearly trek to fish in Wyoming, and we still get together as often as possible. Those connections are a source of joy and refreshment to me and my children. Make every effort to keep your family relationships as consistent as you can. Even though doing that may be hard to work into your schedule and your budget, you and your children will benefit from the comfort and encouragement of a loving, extended family.

DISCOVERING YOUR REAL FRIENDS

A midlife divorce takes its toll on friendships. Because all of us in the Radical group had been married more than 25 years, many of our friendships were couple friends or friends from our husband's career or friends through our children's activities. These groups have a hard time figuring out what to do with us during and after the divorce. And at some point our children go off to college, and we don't have those kid-connections any longer.

Relationships with friends change. Friends try hard not to take sides. Friends try to be there for both of you. Deep in your heart you wonder why friends want to maintain a relationship with a person who has lied to everyone—either directly or indirectly, had a long-term affair, and been instrumental in breaking up two families. Just accept the fact that they will, and they do.

I think mostly friends are trying to be supportive, and they are trying not to be judgmental, and maybe some feel they shouldn't get involved because they don't know the whole story. Remember, they are in a difficult position. One of our close couple friends has remained supportive of both my ex-husband and me. They encouraged and nurtured me in countless ways. They let my husband stay in their extra room until he found an apartment. But I think the whole situation has been hard on them. They are trying to be loyal to both of us.

Some friends worried that if they did something with me, they would offend my ex-husband and vice versa. So sometimes I think they avoided both of us. Some friends still needed the connection with my ex-husband for referrals. Time with friends is often hard to find, so if there is an excuse not to make the effort, some people just take the easy way out, I think, and call someone else—someone not so complicated. I am forever grateful to those friends who took the bold step of getting involved. Remember that when friends of yours need encouragement.

In our age group, many of the Radical Women had put our own educations or careers on hold to help our husbands with their careers. Many of us helped our partner through medical school or dental school or hosted corporate parties to help him move up the ladder. Most of us were stay-at-home moms, and many of us felt that our main job was to help our husbands and take care of our families. That's what I wanted to do, and even though I had the benefit of having work to do that I could do from home, I was a stay-at-home mom until our divorce.

Being a full-time wife and mother is a wonderful family-strengthening and society-enhancing job, but often that role didn't leave much room for our own personal pursuits. Even though all of us had individual women friends, friends from church, friends from groups like book clubs, health clubs, and neighbors, much of our social life revolved around our husbands and our children. I have always enjoyed that. I liked helping my husband. I like being a mother. I like doing things for my family. I like making our home a place of refreshment and fun, and I consider it a launching pad for all sorts of family accomplishments.

Almost every woman in the Radical group had been a stay-at-home mom—the result of our age and what was going on when we got married. Most of us were in our early 20s when we married and had children shortly thereafter.

My husband and I traveled with a group for about 20 years, but because it involved his profession, I suddenly was left out of that. His golfing buddies, and my friends as well, had a tournament every year after which the guys and their wives got together for a potluck dinner. I was left out of that. All of the hospital get-togethers or the medical practice parties with fellow physicians and their spouses suddenly included the new woman instead of me. I was devastated. And lonely. And unsure of myself as a person. I cried every time I knew they were having a party or going on a trip without me. I pictured everyone having a great time without a second thought about me. It made me feel insignificant, dispensable and miserable.

But as hard as it has been, I have had to accept being replaced by my husband's new girlfriend in those social gatherings. During the first travel club trip that I missed, after 20 years of trips, I cried most of the weekend. I pictured my ex-husband and his girlfriend and all of "our" friends laughing and having a great time. I wondered if anyone even missed me at all.

I remembered other men in the group who had gone through the midlife crazies. One doctor with seven children divorced his wife of 38 years and showed up with a young babe on his arm. (He later married her, and she is younger than several of his children.) I always tried to keep my distance with those women, but over the years it got somehow easier to accept their presence and be cordial, even though I never got very close to any of them. I knew that's what would happen with my friends.

I knew that time and distance and the progression of life would mean that eventually I would be replaced in that fun group. That made me despondent, depressed and just sick at heart. One wonderful person from that group called before one spring trip and said, "We wish he and his girlfriend would stay home, and you could come with us." That simple phone call made my day. I still receive cards and notes from people in that group, and have visited several of those friends in their hometowns, but I still miss our trips together.

All in all, I felt as if many lifelong friends suddenly were gone. In reality, even though the big social connections were gone, my real friends didn't go anywhere. It just took determined effort to find time to get together, and it's not easy. Regardless of the specific circumstances, all of the Radical Women had to figure out some way to maneuver the social minefield after divorce. We all had to figure out how to reconnect with those people we cared about. And let me warn you, in *many* cases you have to take the initiative. Most couple friends just want the whole situation to go away.

I sometimes think if there were more negative consequences from friends, husbands might think twice about leaving their family. Maybe not, but I think if my ex-husband's golfing buddies early on had said, "As long as you're having this affair, find someone else to play golf with. When you get a divorce or get your life back on the right track, call us. Until then, find another foursome."

The Bible says, "You are not to keep company with anyone who claims to be a Christian brother but indulges in sexual sins, or is greedy, or is a swindler, or worships idols, or is a drunkard or abusive. Don't even eat lunch with such a person." That's harsh, but maybe it would make a difference.

Anyway, friends usually can't do that, especially male friends. I think my husband's friends hoped to help him, and me, in some way by staying connected. Female friends seem to have less difficulty making a stand. Maybe in the back of their minds, they think, "That could be me." In reality, if I, and our children, couldn't make my husband change his actions, his golfing group probably couldn't either. But I know that at least he would have had second thoughts on Wednesday afternoons when it was time to tee off.

Over the weeks, months and years, I have maintained a relationship with many of our close friends on my own. I might not get to see them as often as I would like, and I am not invited to the medical parties or retirement celebrations, but those friends still call. We still go to dinner, and I still feel as if they care about me. Friends sent serious and funny cards, had me over for dinner or a basketball game, listened to me, cried with me, held me while I cried, and grieved with me through the whole ordeal. My wonderful friend in California let me veg-out (does *anyone* still use that word?) at her house for a few days and didn't make any demands on me, except to let her take care of me at her house near the beach.

My best friend from high school invited me to her house in Atlanta, and we ate delicious Southern food and caught up in one weekend after years apart. She sat next to me and let me cry all the way through services at her church. Let your friends help. They are like water in the desert. They make you feel worthy again after long dry months of feeling like you are the biggest failure in the universe.

My friends were an unbelievable support, but I understand that many of the friends in our own town are in a difficult situation. Many of them don't really know the whole story. Divorce is so common these days people might not think that much about it. Many of my husband's also-divorced buddies simply had a new guy to play more golf with. In the Radical Women group, we all fought to save our marriages, but in the end we were just one in the long list of divorces printed every week in the newspaper, and because of that we had to redefine and in some cases reestablish every single friendship we had.

> *"Let your friends help. They are like water in the desert. They make you feel worthy again after long dry months of feeling like you are the biggest failure in the universe."*

ABOUT 'SETTING THE RECORD STRAIGHT'

Let me say a word here about "setting the record straight," both with family, especially his, and friends. Don't waste precious time trying to convince people about how terrible your ex-husband was—or is. If either friends or family are willing to maintain a relationship with you, make it as pleasant a prospect as you can. Except for a very few close friends and a few family members, no one else will probably ever understand what really happened.

Especially at the beginning, I was so upset about how this divorce would affect my Christian influence that I wanted to make sure people knew I had no other option. I wanted friends and family to know that I tried everything to keep our marriage together. I wanted them to know that I think marriage is a sacred trust that cannot be dissolved lightly or just because of some minor disagreements. I was afraid people might think I thought this whole situation was okay. In reality, I didn't think any of it was okay, and I wanted to make sure everyone knew that. Friends deserve to know the truth, but don't beat them over the head with it day after day.

Some friends and acquaintances don't want to hear the ugly details, and his family, especially, will always primarily hear his side of it, however erroneous and lopsided it is. Don't try to convert them to your version of the truth. You will just set yourself up for more heartache and grief. If you must, tell your side as calmly and as truthfully as you can, and then move on. Some will listen but will never really accept your interpretation of events, anyway. Just face that. They are probably hearing a completely different story from him. In reality, the people you really care about will know what happened. What happens from now on is of more importance to everyone. If all you do is complain about how sad your lot in life is and how terrible he was, they most likely won't go out of their way to have you in their future at all. It's not fair, but not many other people will ever know what he really did, and you could never really describe it if you tried, so give up trying to tell them every chance you get.

I had two amazing groups of women friends who supported me through all of this—my book club friends and the swim team moms. The swim team moms were unbelievable and even helped with my daughter's bridal luncheon the morning of her wedding. They got together, helped plan the menu, brought food and were there for me in every way imaginable during that time. All through this ordeal, they, and many of their husbands, were an inspiration in ways they don't even realize. And they were an irreplaceable safety valve for my son. He spent time at most of their houses during this upheaval. They always welcomed him and gave him a break from everything going on at home. I appreciate that more than I can say.

My book club cohorts gave me moral and physical support all along the way with their prayers, hugs and positive strokes. Certain individuals were absolute jewels. They know who they are. Nurture and nourish your women friends, especially now. Maintain those vital, life-saving connections for yourself and for your children as well.

According to research reported by journalist Melissa Healy, "women are keepers of each other's secrets, boosters of one another's wavering confidence, co-conspirators in life's adventures. Through laughter, tears and an inexhaustible river of talk, they keep each other well and make each other better. For women, friendship not only rules, it protects. It buffers the hardships of life's transitions." Those statements are absolutely true through a midlife divorce.

I have always been a fairly independent person. All of the Radical Women seemed to be. But even as nurturing as the book club was, the actual time together was sometimes difficult. Women talk about their families and where they are going with their husbands and about visiting their children in another state or even about some small, wonderful thing their husband did. Almost all books revolve around relationships. I often cried on the way home from those meetings. I envied their stable relationships, the companionship, and the supportive, caring husbands they all seemed to have.

Since my husband was in medicine, I often went to social gatherings by myself because he was on call or dealing with an emergency (or maybe meeting a lonely, dysfunctional employee!). I didn't mind the part about being occasionally alone at a party, but it is completely different when you go to a gathering of swim team or track team parents and everyone else is a couple. In your head they are all perfectly happy, loving couples, and you're not. It's worse when your ex-husband shows up with his skinny, smiling girlfriend. The evening becomes not only awkward, but also a test to see if you can make it through the night without falling apart. I think sometimes I tried too hard to show that I was okay. At other times, I just said "Good night" early and went home. I almost always stopped on a dark street somewhere and cried before I got home.

One night I showed up at the house of one of our swim team friends and pretty much broke down in the kitchen after a party we had both attended. It was pouring down rain, and I sat in their kitchen and cried. I hated seeing my ex-husband who seemed to be having such a great time. I hated that we were not together. I sobbed, "We are supposed to be together! I hate this! Am I going to feel like this forever? Is my heart going to hurt like this forever?"

Deep down I thought I might, but the *real* answer is, "No, you won't feel like this forever." You will, however, feel like this for longer than you want to. You will feel those awful, agonizing feelings for more days and nights than you think you should. For a while, if you are like most of the Radical Women, you will cry after every party. You will go home and lie on your bed staring up at the ceiling and wonder if life is worth the pain. But eventually, you will, in baby steps, get a better grip on things. Then finally, finally, finally one day, you will actually go to some social occasion and have a decent time. I know you can't believe this early on, but those utterly lost and sad emotions will ever so slowly begin to fade away. But I have to be honest. From where you are now, just starting out this process of healing, don't even think about how long it will be until you feel really better. It's too depressing.

Here's some Radical advice for dealing with friends. As with your children, let your couple friends have space to deal with the situation as they need to. Let them know you value their friendship. Understand when they invite your husband, and even his girlfriend, to their get-togethers. It's best to try not to think about it, because it will make you lonely and sad. I would get these ridiculous pictures in my head about what fun they were all having together. Speaking from experience, those images bring on an agony of defeat that is hard to describe. Try to think about something else.

Don't be afraid to call and ask if friends want to go to dinner, even though sometimes during this journey you wonder if you *are* any fun or if there is something inherently wrong with you, and maybe your friends don't really like you either.

For a while, I was so dejected and sad, even calling anyone took too much energy. I was barely able to get myself through the long days and lonely nights. But as hard as it is, try to stay in touch with the people you care about. Talk about your situation when you need to, but don't bad-mouth your ex-husband day after day, week after week, month after month. In fact, sometimes don't talk about your situation at all when you are with them. In the beginning they will talk about it, and you can talk about it, but after awhile even our closest friends want us to move on. And we do sound ugly and depressing if we just continually dwell on how sad we are, or how hurt we are, or how hard this is.

Our good friends know how difficult it is. They will be patient with us—for a while. And it's not as if you can never bring up the divorce or your ex-husband, but when you feel stronger and when you can, get back to life. Talk about current events or a movie or an interesting book you're reading or, if you're really desperate, even politics or religion! Convey some of the life lessons you're learning through this—and no, not just how pathetic midlife crisis men are or how ridiculous your ex-husband is acting. Keep those observations to yourself.

FINDING A SUPPORT NETWORK

In an attempt to stay connected, all of the Radical Women eventually tried some form of singles group meeting, either a support group at a church or a community outreach for singles. Some of the support groups were worth the time, but all of us had horror stories about some singles event.

One of the Radical Women said, "Can you imagine anything worse than a 'Singles Hoedown' at the community center? Can you imagine anything more desperate?" The one formal support group I attended seemed to be full mostly of older, somewhat hopeless women. I realize I didn't give them a fair chance, but I never went back. I did find a regular, not just for singles, Sunday school group and another small study group at church whose members were unbelievably open, receptive and helpful. At this point most of us were not ready to be pigeonholed as a single. We just want to be our pre-divorce, fun, confident, happy selves.

I for one didn't want to be singled out for my failures with a group of other failures. That's not the correct way to think, but at the time, I thought it just the same. And it seems as though some people get addicted to the group, to reliving all the pain and anguish and retelling the same sad, sad story. Groups aren't for everyone. So, if your group is stuck on reliving the past and the pain and not providing positive solutions, definitely find another group.

Sometimes even having a brother or sister or one close friend to talk things over with is enough. For me, I just wanted to feel better, and friends, family and our loose-knit Radical group were just what I needed. I know of other women who have been encouraged and strengthened by various support groups. Just be careful that your group is helping you move forward and not helping you stay stuck.

"Just be careful that your group is helping you move forward and not helping you stay stuck."

Getting reconnected is tough and complex. You aren't just reconnecting; you are establishing completely new relationships. In a sense some facets of your relationship with your children are new. You are forging new ways of doing things and creating new traditions. You will have a new relationship with your extended families. With your friends. With your community. In a way, you are a new person. You have a brand new chance to be who you want to be. I know at first all you want to be is married. Or be part of a couple. But you have more to offer than that. You have a full, rich, abundant, exciting life ahead of you that is more than being someone's wife.

Find a group or someone to whom you can talk openly and freely. You won't need that support forever, but you do need it in the beginning. Our Radical group was a tremendous help to me from the very first night we met. I told my counselor before that first meeting that I wasn't sure I was up to any group commitment yet, much less leading one, because I felt so weak myself.

I didn't see how I could help anyone, and I might just start crying without doing anything good at all. She encouraged me to start the group anyway because, "they are all probably feeling the same things," and she said we could find encouragement from each other wherever we were on the journey to recovery. She was right.

I discovered that I had so much in common with every woman who came. We were all a bit tentative in committing to the group in the beginning, and one woman who really needed to come just never could muster up the courage to do so. She said, "I feel like I would just fall apart and have nothing to give to the group at this point." I told her we all felt like that. She never came to the meetings. She is a great, fun person, and I know we could have all benefited from her input, and I'm still sorry she didn't join us. I learned important lessons and gained new insight every time the group met.

We all knew what the others around the table were going through. We laughed together. We talked about solutions together. And even though the Radical rules specified that these were not sessions to talk about how terrible our ex-husband was, sometimes we couldn't help ourselves! The meetings were also not to be pity parties where we could just moan and groan about how terrible and sad and hard and unfair our lives were. Anyway, we occasionally did a tiny bit of both of those things we weren't supposed to do.

We all had stories about some ridiculous thing our ex-significant other had done, and we usually ended up laughing about them because some of them were just unbelievable. We also talked about some of the dumb, ridiculous things we ourselves had done. The wonderful thing about the group is that all of these women are in the same boat. You feel comfortable with each other. You can let your guard down and you can let go of your emotions, whatever they are. You find out you are not the only one crying all day or on the verge of criminal action!

Find a group like ours. Make a group of your own. Sadly, I guarantee there are women everywhere going through this same thing. Find them and be your own Radical Group. Figure out your own Radical names. Start creating your own Radical new life.

Four women were part of my Radical group who lived within five minutes walking or driving distance from my house. On more than one occasion, I went to one of their houses and cried or ranted about something that had happened. I never got turned away once, no matter what time I showed up. Invariably they opened their hearts and their homes to me as I did to them.

A neighborhood friend of mine who lost her husband to a brain tumor said to me, "I have a spare room in my house. If you ever need a place to get away—away from your kids or away from your house—just come here. You can shut the door and cry or sleep or whatever. I know how it is. I was trying so hard to be strong for my kids that I needed a place I could just get away and cry." Having that available was a great help. Offer another Radical Woman that option at your home.

Regardless of whether we are talking about family relationships or friends or peripheral groups, the chemistry in all of our social interactions changes because we are no longer a part of a pair. In the beginning every Radical woman I know feels as though she is the one single ship sailing in an endless ocean of couples.

We all need a helping hand from time to time, so don't hesitate to admit that and take advantage of those who truly want to help. Also, think about ways you can help others—either those in this same situation or anyone who needs a little boost.

One of the reasons I believe God allows us to suffer is that it prepares us to help others. In 2 Corinthians Paul says, "What a wonderful God we have. He is the Father of our Lord Jesus Christ, the source of every mercy, and the one who so wonderfully comforts and strengthens us in our hardships and trials. And why does He do this? So that when others are troubled, needing our sympathy and encouragement, we can pass on to them this same help and comfort God has given us." Stay connected and be sensitive to others who need your help, or more correctly, need God's help through you.

CHAPTER SIX

FACE REALITY

*Reality kicks in when you finally
face the fact that your marriage
is really over and you ask
yourself, "What do I do now?"*

Facing reality means accepting the reality of your situation. Most of us have put that off as long as we can.

Most of us deny the hard emotional work we have to go through to do that. Most of us try to ignore the decisions we have to make to take control of our lives. But the beasts of wishful thinking and ignoring reality just keep roaring until they eat us up or we figure out how to deal with them. Facing reality means taking stock of where you are and who you are, now. Where you are is relatively easy. Discovering who you are takes more effort. Getting real is about respecting yourself and appreciating yourself and rediscovering every good thing you are and every good thing you have to offer those around you.

During one of the early stages of my divorce, a friend's husband dropped dead of a heart attack right in the middle of an ordinary day. At the wake and the funeral, I saw her children grieving. I saw her grieving with grace, and I thought, "That would be so much easier than what I'm dealing with." At the funeral, my friend's sons got up and said things about their dad ... about respect, admiration, inspiration and strength of character. They said things about how much he loved their mother. At this point I wondered what my children's feelings would have been about their father if he had just died. Disappointment? Confusion? Anger? And I had no consolation at all. They couldn't have said anything at all about how much he loved me. I cried with my friend at the wake, but I think I was crying as much for myself.

Sitting at that funeral, I thought, "I wish my husband had dropped dead." It wouldn't be as hard to deal with as this rejection. It wouldn't be so embarrassing to explain. It's humiliating to know that he chose a dissatisfied woman, who was not faithful to her own husband, over me and our family—that our 33 years together in the end didn't really mean that much to him. "If he had just died, it wouldn't be as devastating to me and to everything my life has been about."

I expressed these thoughts to a friend, who had been a grief counselor for many years, who said, "With death, it's final. After a certain grieving period, however long that is, you can move on. People give you space and send cards and bring food to your house. Your situation is as painful as a death and in some ways more painful because you have to keep viewing the body over and over and over again. You have to keep dealing with the person who has rejected you. The wounds take longer to heal because there are new injuries all of the time, and unlike a death, people don't give you space to mourn in the same way."

We are expected to be our old selves, and we're trying hard to convince people this doesn't hurt as much as it does. Death is random. Leaving our marriage was a conscious choice my husband willingly made. I hate for people to know that because it is so catastrophic to who I am as a woman.

All of the Radical Women were trying to rediscover who we were without "him." My whole situation made me wonder how valuable I was—if the man I tried most to please thought so little of me that he would throw away every single thing we had built together. It made me question everything about myself—my desirability, my intellect, my spirituality, my sexuality—everything. I had lots of people telling me it wasn't about me, but instead about his insecurities, but that was hard to believe when outwardly he appeared to have no insecurities whatsoever. What I heard from his words and his actions was that I was not enough of a woman for him. At the time, those realities were very hard to deal with, and I cried every time I thought of them.

As Radical Women, we need to accept the hard truth that our marriage is dead and so are many of our dreams. We must jump into the deep, cold water of rebuilding our self-esteem and rediscovering the best of who we are, and who we can be. Even though such introspection can be uncomfortable, it forces us to take stock of ourselves and ask, "Am I being my best self?" If you are like the other Radical Women, this trauma has probably not been your "one shining moment." All of us in the Radical group suffered from low, or non-existent, self-esteem, and our actions have sometimes been embarrassing and destructive.

We all get validation from those around us. Although we each have to develop our own feelings of security and self-sufficiency, we nonetheless get reinforcement about ourselves from the people close to us. And when the person who knows us better than anyone else in the world suddenly tells us by his words and his actions that we aren't enough, it shakes our confidence to the core.

These things are often happening when menopause or perimenopause is making us feel frumpy, sweaty and crazy as well. We wonder if we are who we think we are. I went from feeling self-confident, attractive and fun, to feeling ugly and unsure of myself on just about every level. And I was unbelievably lonely.

After my husband's affair and our separation and divorce, I felt afraid. I was afraid to be fun. I was afraid to be outgoing. I was afraid to be bold. I felt self-conscious, and I worried that I had nothing to offer to other people—men or women. I looked at women whose husbands were faithful, and instead of admiring their husbands for their fidelity, I looked at the wives and thought, "What is she doing that I'm not? Why is her husband faithful to her while my husband has decided that he needs another woman to make life enjoyable?" I asked myself over and over again, "What did I do wrong? What could I have done differently? Why doesn't he love me anymore?"

One day my counselor said to me, "I encourage patients to try to uncover what their part of the problem has been, and you have done that. But enough is enough! When are you going to stop blaming yourself, and start recognizing this for what it is—a lack of honesty and moral integrity on his part? When are you going to hold him accountable for his bad behavior?" A friend asked, "Where is your 'righteous indignation' about this?"

FIGURING OUT 'WHO AM I?'

The Radical Women all worked hard to figure things out, but we have behaved, and still may be behaving, in unbecoming and unproductive ways, and may still be asking the wrong questions. We have all wondered, "What's the matter with me?" "What did I do wrong?" Although there is a place for asking those hard questions and accepting the answers, remember that we are in a place we did not choose, did not want and tried to prevent. You might not have done anything specifically or purposely wrong. The problem may have been more about your ex-husband's failures than with yours. The more appropriate questions to ask today are, "Who am I now?" and "Where do I go from here?"

The Radical Women slowly began to ask different questions. "Can we be doing this recovery any better? Are we doing the things we really need to be doing to get some closure on this and move on?" By getting help from professional counselors and by being at the Radical meetings and by taking physical and emotional care of ourselves, we felt as if we were at least taking the steps to get started. Plus, we reassured ourselves that we were also trying our best to figure out how to help our children and the other people we cared about. So, even though we were moving in fits and starts, we were trying to make the best of this awful situation for ourselves and for the people important to us.

Our husbands, on the other hand, were spreading destruction on every side, apparently without a second thought. Their lives were not only full of a new and exhilarating romantic relationship, but with renewed confirmation and affirmation. Before long that fact started making me mad. Why was I letting myself be dragged down by sadness and heartache and despair, when my husband and his girlfriend seemed oblivious to the devastation and hurt they were leaving in their wake?

One of my friends said, "You know, it's amazing how your husband has just seemed to skate through this whole thing unaffected—without a hitch." His self-esteem, instead of being threatened, seemed to be enhanced. He had an adoring, new girlfriend who made him feel wonderful and desirable and smart and sexy. He had a wife who tried everything to make him give up his girlfriend and come back to the family. What more could a guy want? He had two women who desperately wanted him. While he was basking in the admiration of his new love, I was curled up in my bed at night wondering what I did wrong. I was sick at heart that my husband wanted to leave our family and live with someone else. In looking back from where I am now, I think, "What in the world was I doing?" But at the time, I couldn't seem to help myself.

After developing strategies to deal with the day-to-day basics of getting through this ordeal, the Radical Women started trying to figure out, "Okay, I'm still standing, what now? Who am I now? What comes next? I'm not anyone's wife. I'm not Mrs. Anybody. However, I am still a mother and grandmother, sister, daughter, friend, member of a church, and citizen of my community."

The big question in all that, of course, is "Who am I for myself?" That is not an easy question. It's a lot easier when everything in your life is going well. But when virtually everything you hold dear is in jeopardy, you desperately need the real you to step up. The new independent you has to show her stuff, to show what she's made of. Believe me, that is worse than scary.

I lay awake at night trying to figure out who I really was. I thought, "What if I discover I'm nothing on my own? What if I can't support myself? What if I can't pay the bills? What if I never have a date? What if the kids think he's more fun and want to live with him? What if no one likes me? What if I feel this sad, sick ache in my heart forever?"

Valuing Your Independence

First of all, one bit of advice that is very difficult—but is good advice just the same. In the beginning of trying to discover the person you want to be, try to learn to accept the good things about being single. Make the most of your independence. Treasure your new-found freedom. Now, from several years out, I can advise that, but even as I write those words, I know how ridiculous that is to even ask in the beginning. Personally, I hated every single thing about being a single—about being in that horrible, sad group of middle-aged divorced women.

I hated most of all losing the family of my dreams. I hated sleeping alone. I hated the loss of companionship. I hated what it did to our children and grandchildren and everyone else. I hated eating alone. I hated the financial position it put me in. I hated making decisions about the house and the car. I hated sharing our children with him and his girlfriend. I hated that sex was gone from my life. I could go on and on about everything I hated about being single. And I consider myself to be a strong, independent woman.

During this time, I cried at church sitting in the pew by myself. I cried after parties because I hated being there by myself because my husband didn't love me anymore. If you haven't figured it out, I cried a lot, as did the majority of all of the other Radical Women at first. Most likely, you're doing that, too. That's all right for now. But eventually, you have to stop crying and feeling sorry for yourself and figure out how to move on.

Even though I've said you should recognize the good things about being single, I'll admit I struggled through every social situation that first year. I remember going by my son's house after a party not long after the divorce was final. The party was given by a dear friend who was trying her best to include me in social activities; it was an innocuous "Girls Night Out" for champagne and chocolate and to watch the Academy Awards. I left the party early because several of the women were also divorced and were making those "divorced woman" comments about various actors' physical attributes. Suddenly I was devastated about being divorced and being in that category, the category of women who "weren't worth loving" anymore.

I stopped by our oldest son's house, and when I could finally speak, I sobbed into the sofa, "I hate this! I don't want to be divorced! I'll never get over this!" When I first walked in, I was so upset that he and his wife thought something terrible had happened like a car wreck or being robbed. In my opinion, catastrophes like that would have been easy compared to the mental anguish I was going through at that moment.

Our first counselor told my husband, "The emotional wounds caused by your actions are more painful than if you stabbed her with a knife." I can honestly say that was true for me that night of the Academy Awards. The pain was very real and physically debilitating. I wondered if I would ever recover.

During that first year after the divorce, I went to the wedding of a friend whose first husband had died a few years earlier. I sat with other book club members and their husbands and made it through the wedding, even the vows (during which, of course, I was reliving my own vows), but had to leave during the reception. I was sick at heart that I had no one to share the celebration and the night with.

Later in the year, I also went to the wedding of a wonderful young man who had been a friend for twenty years. I always felt a special closeness to him and his family and wanted very much to be at his wedding.

I drove to Colorado by myself and stayed with my son's wife's parents in Denver, and I went to the wedding by myself. The simple outdoor ceremony was beautiful and unique even to the white doves flying away at the end. However, once the music for the reception started, and after a dance that my son graciously asked me to share, I had to leave. I found a quiet dark room and just sat there until the tears stopped, and I could compose myself—probably half an hour or more. I then said my goodbyes and drove home.

I have always loved weddings. I love the family connections and having all ages of people dancing and celebrating together. That night, I didn't delight in being single. I didn't enjoy my independence. All I wanted was my husband to dance with at our friend's wedding. So believe me, I know what I'm asking when I ask you to value singleness. It is not easy!

The Radical Women wish we had a magic pill to make it easier for you, but we don't. So, even if you can't identify with this concept very well right now, remember for future reference that there are some definite positives about being on your own. It's just that from where you are at this moment, they are *very* hard to see.

Even though you don't feel like it, you are growing stronger through these experiences. You are going through that difficult stage of standing alone, of learning how to be alone, of really putting yourself in God's hands. Even though it is hard to do at first, try to focus on the people around you. Try to give encouragement and attention to others. Direct your energy on finding out about them, about what's going on in their lives. All of these things are easier said than done, I know. These are not easy lessons. All we can say is, "Hang on. Don't give up. Keep trying."

One good thing about your new position in life is that you may have more time for your children and grandchildren, for your friends, for your church, for extracurricular activities. The only trouble is, for a while you are in so much pain that it is hard to make those relationships and activities what they should be. You just have to bumble through the best you can for now. Pray that God will give you a light heart and a joyful outlook when you are interacting with others. I was praying, and I was trying, but some days I was simply too sad.

REDEFINING YOUR LIFE

Your unwanted midlife divorce forces you to stop and take stock of yourself. One of the disguised blessings of this situation is that you have an opportunity to redefine yourself and your life. You are forced to think about what you really want for the rest of your life.

In a *Time* magazine article called "Midlife Crisis? Bring It On! How women of this generation are seizing that stressful, pivotal moment in their lives to reinvent themselves," women are encouraged to look at this time as an unexpected gift. The article says that when midlife hurdles—whether divorce or disease or empty nest or the death of a parent—hit, "women are figuring out how to turn these sometimes traumatic, treacherous times born of sorrow or stress into opportunities."

Your desires may have changed. Your dreams may be different. Or your goals may be brand new. You can take another look at some passion that you did not have a chance to develop earlier in your life. Take advantage of this opportunity to explore what you really want.

In some long-term marriages, both partners may be coasting, just plodding along in a not-so-exciting status quo. You have a God-given chance to use all of your life experiences and maturity to choose the life you *really* want. You have a fresh chance to shine! Not one thing is stopping you. You can go after any dream you choose.

Realistically, many women are stuck in that horrible house of ho-hum. One thing is certain. Your life right now is not ho-hum! A life change has been forced upon you, so grab the chance and make something wonderful of it! Make something incredible out of the rest of your hours and days and years!

In the process of rebuilding your self-esteem, don't try to hurry yourself into "getting out there." People encourage us to socialize, and you should try to at least get to the coffee shop or have lunch with a friend or go to book club or whatever. But don't feel pressured to "find someone." Most of us in the beginning aren't even thinking of finding anyone, we're trying to survive; but somewhere in the back of our minds we worry that time is running out especially if we are in our 50s like most of us are.

> *"Enjoy getting to know yourself. Your real self. Take time to discover who you are and what you really like and what you want the rest of your life to look like."*

Regardless of that sometimes demoralizing reality, don't force yourself to look for a new relationship. Take the time you need to stabilize and heal first. It will be better for everyone. Forget about what your ex is doing. Think, instead, about what you want to happen in your own life. Sometimes Radical Women rush into new relationships because they are lonely. Children are gone. You may not have a job, and your husband is basking in a wonderful new life. But just step back and take a deep breath. Cry if you have to, but realize that the future is up to you, and it can be wonderful.

Enjoy getting to know yourself. Your *real* self. Take time to discover who you are and what you really like and what you want the rest of your life to look like. Realize that loneliness is hard and sad, but it's temporary, and it can help you focus on what you want for yourself. Some women decide they would rather stay single, and in the end don't want to give up their new-found independence and freedom. Others get involved in a caring outreach or go back to school or start a new business.

A recent *Wall Street Journal* article, "Women Often Discover Their Business Talent After Kids Are Raised," says women can blossom in all kinds of new ways after they are finished raising their children. It tells of a 47-year-old woman who now owns her own Denver marketing firm, saying, "...she suffered a string of losses: Both her parents died, her marriage dissolved and, for a time, her sons went to live with their father. 'I had no money, no job, no family,' she says, 'But I started confronting everything about myself, and I decided I can't feel afraid anymore. I'm going to feel joy, I'm going to feel prosperous and I'm not wasting another minute.'" That's the attitude we need.

Take a deep breath and rediscover yourself. Enjoy yourself. Recognize your own unique value and reestablish your sense of the wonderful person you are on your own. Keep reminding yourself that, if you let it, life will be good again. And God, if you let him, will give you a victory beyond imagining.

Go to the library or bookstore or go online and find the resources you need to figure out your next step. Tap into a human resource counselor or a life coach who will help you discover your innate strengths and natural abilities. I have a friend who is a life coach who sat down with me on several occasions and helped me take stock of where I was and helped me decide where I actually wanted to be. In the past you probably had obligations and made choices based on early life circumstances. You may still have some obli-gations, but you also may have more flexibility. Give up trying to make things like they were when you were married. Start fresh! God lets us have a new start every single day.

Have a conference with your children and tell them some of your new hopes and dreams. Let them be a part of your enthusiasm. Reassure them that you are not planning to go off to Timbuktu, but do let them know you are looking at some inspiring new alternatives. I think most of our children would be thrilled to catch a glimmer of a confident mother who is excited about the future. You can consciously find a joy-filled purpose for your life, and you can formulate a plan to fulfill that purpose. You can choose a future that embraces your inner longings and yearnings and enhances your personal strengths and capabilities. Start that process now.

I remember the day my divorce was final. My wise attorney said, "Many women discover all kinds of new things about themselves through this." At that moment, standing in the October sunshine on the courthouse steps, I was trying desperately not to cry and thinking to myself, "I don't want to discover anything new about myself. I just want to grow old with my husband and enjoy our grandchildren together and do all the fun things that this time in life brings." But right now, if you are reading this book, as hard as it is to face, the fact is you are not going to grow old with your husband. He wants something else, and you can't do anything about that. So, you're going to have to figure out a new life. You can make it wonderful. It may not seem possible right now, and it takes courage and determination, but you absolutely can do it—and your life can be an amazing, incredible, absolutely better-than-you-can-even-envision triumph!

This very moment, begin to seriously take stock of what you enjoy. Explore areas that fascinate you. Discover your own particular passions and priorities. You have a brand new chance to use your potential for good in this world in your own unique way. We can each take this situation that started out in our perception as a tragedy and turn it into a launching pad for a whole new life of fulfilling and fun—yes! fun!—contributions to the ultimate good of ourselves, our families, our extended relationships and even our world. We are young, healthy, and bright enough to make a real impact, starting now. And we each have the privilege of deciding how we want to do that.

Rekindle your sense of humor, which I'm sure has been notably absent of late. It might be hiding, but it's still there. I remember after our divorce I went to a celebration party of the swim team parents after the state swim meet. My ex-husband was there, too, of course, having a wonderful time. At one point in the evening, someone told about an article in the paper about authorities finding a certain important part of the male anatomy—frozen—in the front yard of a house in a nearby neighborhood! With a straight face, I asked if there was an address listed. At the moment, I didn't think it was *that* funny, but everyone fell down laughing, and it felt great! People from the swim team still bring that up occasionally.

Just try to relax and be yourself and realize how fun, worthy and worthwhile you still are. Part of who you are is someone who enjoys life and has not forgotten how to laugh and see the funny side of things, even now.

At one event, a longtime friend and his wife and I were talking, and he said something about my ex-husband and me "growing up together." I laughed, and said, "At least one of us grew up!" That comment wouldn't get me on a late-night TV show for being a great comedienne, but it lightened the tone and put everyone more at ease, I think. Remember, people like the old you, and they want to see the old you, so try to find her again whenever you can. Even this horrible situation does create some admittedly funny scenarios. Particularly in the beginning, though, those are hard to see ... especially through the sobs and the tears.

Start thinking about all the things you're good at. Think about the activities you enjoy. Think about your special talents. Take an aptitude test. Take the "spiritual gifts inventory" at church. Try something completely new that sounds exciting. Start trying to visualize how you want your future to look. Formulate what you would like for your day-to-day life to look like in one year or in two years. Or five. Then start doing things every day to make that vision come true.

You have the freedom to do what you want with your life. Most likely your children are fairly independent by now. You have more flexibility. You can stay late at work to finish a challenging project. You can take a night class. You can enroll in an art class. Think about all the intriguing possibilities before you.

Even though you have a whole new world to discover and explore, in reality right now you probably don't like doing that by yourself. But the fact is, you are not part of a couple now. It takes a while to come to grips with that reality. It's not what you planned, but it's what you have, so you are going to have to learn not only to survive it, but figure out a way to grow and blossom because of it. Take the reins and relight that fire of joy about who you are. Be brave. Be adventurous. Rent some movies with strong, win-against-the-odds themes. Read the astounding stories of victory in the Bible. Be courageous enough to put thoughts of inferiority and failure behind you. You, like all of us, have made mistakes, but you are not a failure. Right this minute, you are an amazing woman and a success story waiting to happen.

WHO FAILED, ANYWAY?

To put things in perspective, just think for a minute about whether these men sound like great success stories.

In our Radical group, my husband decided a younger, unhappily-married woman was his new love. (He's now with someone else). One ex-husband has never paid any alimony or child support and has not seen his children in more than six years. (No one knows where he is). One ex-husband decided that a new woman from Greece was the woman to bring him lifelong joy. (He's now with his second someone else). A big company CEO decided after 27 years and two beautiful daughters and grandchildren that he "had never really been in love with his wife," but now was really in love with a redhead he had met at a party. (She is two years older than his youngest daughter). A local entertainer decided that alcohol, drugs and groupies were more fun than staying with his wife and children. (He's with someone different and younger all the time). An article about him in our paper quoted him saying that he was down to high-school or college girls now as his partners—and he thought that was funny.

As the Radical Women sat around the table, as much as it appeared to the outside world that we had failed, we knew that even though we had made our share of mistakes through our years of marriage, we had not forced our husbands to make these choices. They made them themselves. And if anyone had failed to make good life decisions, they did.

In fact, the insecure men who fall into the trap of midlife romances are the subject of jokes and are looked at with a certain disdain. On the surface they may seem to have the best of all worlds and suffer few real consequences. Our society has come to accept infidelity and the resulting divorce without much surprise.

The men and their new women appear to do great. Friends seem to bend over backwards to be open-minded. Families try their best to make the new relationship work for everyone. But deep down, people don't really respect these men. People think about them with an undercurrent of disapproval. Most women think of them with something like disgust. The following is from a letter to me from a friend of more than 30 years. His disappointment is apparent:

"...I have wonderful memories of all the great and crazed times we had together in med school, and he always seemed devoted to you and your family. I guess we all know of people who have these divorces after they are in their mid-50s and universally it completely fouls up their lives ... plus the negative impact on the lives of their spouses, children and friends.... There is always the potential to stray from one's commitment to your spouse—for both men and women—and to your children and grandchildren, but at our ages if we haven't achieved the perspective and values to know the relative importance of family, tradition, and appropriateness in life then there is a grave imbalance in our judgment and maturity. I can only feel sorry for him as life will never be as smooth and serene, nor as complete, as the life that he has left.

"It must be a blow to one's self esteem to have to deal with the 'other woman,' but I hope that you realize that this is not a manifestation of your inadequacy, but the product of (his) inability to be comfortable in his own masculinity.

"It must be a blow to one's self esteem to have to deal with the 'other woman,' but I hope that you realize that this is not a manifestation of your inadequacy, but the product of his inability to be comfortable in his own masculinity. He certainly is not alone in this state as we both know men who can't be satisfied with the adoration of just one woman. Unfortunately, it is a disease that is never satisfied and continues to replicate itself, which may satisfy the temporary desire to be reassured about one's attractiveness but never leads to true fulfillment and completeness...."

While most decent people feel the same as the opinion voiced above, some people are afraid to stand up for what they know deep in their hearts is right and hesitate to voice that opinion.

Making things even more difficult, most of our ex-husbands do everything they can to be great guys in their new relationships. One ex-husband cheerily said to one of his four biological children, "I have seven children now!" I'm sure those *new* children are loving the financial support and caring attention he graciously bestows on them.

Another dad is going to walk his girlfriend's daughter down the aisle when she gets married because "she admires him so much." When his biological daughter asked the girl why she admired him so much, she said because her own father had run off with another woman and left their family. She had no idea this new father figure had done the same thing. To her he had turned on all the charm of a wonderful, caring, sensitive, honorable man.

In the meantime those of us who had been with these men through all those early days and lean years and children growing years are the ones left to pick up the pieces. Our biological children have to wonder where they're going to fit into his *new* life with his girlfriend or his *new* wife and his *new* children.

CHOOSING TO BE HONORABLE

However, the big question we need to ask ourselves at this point has nothing to do with our ex-husbands. It has everything to do with us. Let your ex-husband's girlfriend or new wife figure out how to deal with someone who does not keep his promises. Let his new wife wonder where he is in the middle of the night when he says he is on call or working late at the office. Let his new girlfriend wonder whom he is really thinking about when he comes to bed at night. Be thankful you don't have to worry about those things anymore.

Be thankful that you can choose to have people in your life who are honest and honorable. But even more important, choose to be honest and honorable yourself. Choose to live right regardless of what those around you are doing. Choose to make loving, good decisions, especially now. Make choices that are good for you, your children, your family and your friends. Choose to have integrity. Choose to look at the good side of life and to make the best of your opportunities. Choose to be the good, strong capable woman you were made to be. And have fun!

Here's a personal story that will help. Earlier, I told of taking an antidepressant that made me so sick physically, emotionally and every other way possible that I honestly was not sure I would survive. It was a horrible night. My internist, and friend, called my family in another city. As I said, my older brother was there by later that night. He had been a great help to me because he had been through a situation much like mine except that his wife was the one who wanted out of the marriage. In the beginning, he had agonized through the experience, but had learned many valuable lessons along the way that he shared with me.

Keep in mind that I have two amazing brothers who helped sustain me throughout this ordeal—my younger brother providing the steady voice of godly wisdom, and my older brother speaking the clear, deep truth of experience. And they are both very spiritual and very funny!

On this occasion my older brother generously came to stay with me for a few days. It was late when he arrived, and I was in bed trying to keep from throwing up and trying to get some sleep while all I could see behind my eyelids was a dark despair. He pretty much left me alone that night.

The next morning, he sat me down and made me look him in the eyes. I was completely embarrassed that I was doing so poorly with this whole situation. For one thing, I am a Christian, and for another I had always considered myself a strong, independent person.

Regardless of how I was feeling, he said without smiling, "Okay. You have a choice to make. You can either let this situation destroy you, or you can see what blessings God can bring out of it, and you can make something fantastic of your life. It's your choice. No one else can decide for you. You have twenty-four hours. You can build a bonfire in the backyard and howl at the moon. You can go to the church building and pray all night. You can call all of your friends and counselors and get advice. You can do whatever you want for the next twenty-four hours. But by tomorrow morning at this time, I want a decision."

Even though I had been trying to make the best of things, and had been trying to see what God was doing in the situation, my brother's ultimatum brought home that the future was up to me. The simple choice was this: I could have a miserable life feeling sorry for myself and reliving every terrible thing my ex-husband had done, or I could have a wonderful life. But whatever future I ended up with, it was going to be my choice. I am so thankful I had someone in my life at that precise moment who could make the alternatives so clear.

At some point, you're going to have to make that clear-cut decision, too.

Realize right now that how the rest of your life turns out is up to you. All the Radical Women know that what you've been through makes you feel insecure and unlovable and unlovely. We've all been there. Get over that! Keep in mind that your ex-husband and his girlfriend are the unlovely, pathetic ones right now—not you—unless you are acting in unlovely, pathetic ways yourself.

That may not be the politically correct thing to say, or the Hollywood take on the situation, but deep down, you know that is true. Their behavior is not cool. It's not glamorous. Having an affair that destroys your marriage is not honorable by any standards. It's selfish and sad and ugly despite the fulfilling and fun scenarios Hollywood, television and music usually portray. But there is absolutely nothing you can do about that except determine not to let this situation defeat you. You have the power to learn from it, grow with it, and become the person God means for you to be because of it. And, you may not believe this, but your situation carries with it the potential for an absolutely amazing new life. Really!

The process begins by appreciating the miracle that is you. Start right now this very minute. Close your eyes and thank God for making you the unique, competent, fun, glorious, real woman that you are.

CHAPTER SEVEN

CHOOSE TO CHANGE

Try this test:
See how much fun it is or how
much good it does to focus on
how miserable you are.
If the answer is 'none,'
try something else.

Probably like you, most of the Radical Women in our group have spent the last 25 or 30 years seeing to the needs of others—our husbands, our children, and maybe now our aging parents. We often haven't taken, or been given, the luxury of maximizing our own unique abilities and talents. Even though we did not want to be divorced in midlife, we can use being in this place to our advantage, not just for us, but for the people in our range of influence.

Beginning right now, we can learn to actually appreciate the potential in this moment. We can learn to focus for once on our own needs, our own special desires, our own private dreams. This new chance to choose our future does not mean that we ignore the needs of those we love and those around us. It does mean, however, that you let yourself shine.

You may feel that your light is dim right now or that you don't have much to share. I want to assure you that you are wrong. Your life now is all about how you view your reality, and you can shine!

CHANGING YOUR SELF TALK

The reality of our life at any given moment has a lot to do with our self talk—what we're saying to ourselves about the situation.

Here's an example. You can say to yourself, "I hate this situation. I hate what my ex-husband has done. I'll never be happy again. I'm going to get even. I don't have enough money. This whole thing really makes me furious."

Or we can talk to ourselves in a more positive way. You can say, instead, "I'm going to learn something worthwhile from this situation. I am extremely blessed to have wonderful children. I'll create the richest, most fulfilling life I can from here on out. I will let the natural laws of reaping and sowing take effect for both my ex-husband and me. The amount of money I have won't be the determining factor in my level of happiness. I'll find new joys that I might not have otherwise discovered."

Your situation hasn't changed a bit, but how you talk and think about it has. Your attitude about the exact same event can make that event either negative or positive. Positive is way better. Negative talk and negative thinking do nothing but make you miserable, and if they go on long enough, they make the people around you miserable, too.

A great newspaper article I ran across by John Boudreau, "It's About Forgiveness," stresses that the wounded *must* not see themselves as victims. The article quotes author Fred Luskin as saying, "If you repeatedly tell your story of pain—he left me for another woman and broke my heart—you are creating a negative narrative that continually wounds you. Telling a different story—I am finally free of a relationship that was not good for me—can move a person from self-pity to confidence." Luskin advises people to "become a hero instead of a victim."

Once you realize in your head and in your heart that you are a good, worthy, worthwhile woman—actually, a magnificent, incredible, strong woman!—you can begin to focus on what you want to do with the rest of your life.

OWNING YOUR FUTURE

I know that if you are reading this book as a newly-divorced or almost-divorced woman, you have a lot of ground to cover before you are ready to really embrace the unbelievable possibilities of the future. The Radical Women all know that. We understand that you may be in the stage where you feel only pain, and see no possibility for the good things that await you. We've all been there. Be patient with yourself. Don't think that you can get through this without the difficult steps of mourning, but do get in your head that a real transformation is on its way. It will be as liberating as the often-used example of a caterpillar morphing into a butterfly.

Last week, two of my grandchildren were expectantly watching and waiting for something to emerge from a grey and dusty cocoon. The coming out of the beautiful yellow and black butterfly finally happened, and, no matter how many times you see it or how old you are, that experience is still breathtaking and miraculous. That same awe-inspiring transformation can happen to you.

Believe me when I say, "The possibilities for what lies ahead in your life are limitless." Remember, too, that you are at a crossroads. You will be making decisions that affect how your future unfolds. You may think the future is out of your hands. The truth is that the future is in your hands in many ways, and you can decide that it will be glorious and magnificent.

Right now, you may think that your life doesn't have much promise because of your financial situation. Financial problems as a single woman can be tough, but all kinds of research shows that after basic needs are met, more money doesn't necessarily mean more happiness. Lack of money can be a motivator to get our most important priorities to the forefront.

For the record, just come to grips with the fact that your ex-husband's life-style will probably not change that much. In fact, most men do better than ever. Many of our husbands built or bought new houses for their new families. In fact, while our ex-husbands are trying to impress their new families with money, gifts and things, most of the Radical Women had to make big changes—more changes than we could deal with well.

Many of us will sell our houses and move to something much smaller. Most of us will need to find some way or some additional way to support ourselves. Most of us will make major lifestyle downshifts, especially in the beginning. But in the midst of all these changes, we also have choices. The main choice is the most important one. We can choose to make the one change that makes all the difference—that makes everything new and full of promise.

We can change our attitude.

We can discover and accept the good things about where we are right now. I admit that in the middle of your struggle, the changes seem overwhelming, and they aren't changes you chose. They have been forced on you by circum-stances that you have little or no control over. Regardless of what changes you are asked to make, you have the power to transform them into some-thing good. Something positive. Something incredible. I know that's hard to believe, but it's true.

I had lunch with one of the members of the first Radical group not long ago, and she said, "I still sometimes get discouraged when I know he is building a new house on the beach with a full-time caretaker for his new girlfriend and her daughter. I can't even take a vacation without finding my own substitute for my classroom."

She has renewed her teaching certificate and is a high school art teacher. Her ex-husband is a surgeon. She said, "I have to watch every penny." She has two kids in college and one in high school, and her ex-husband complains about finances and the extra expenses that sometimes come up with kids that age.

Occasionally, even when we are trying to move forward, troublesome financial realities or lonely social situations still raise their ugly heads. I know unfair circumstances are hard to accept. But as my older brother told me, "Okay, it's unfair. You still have to deal with it. Just because it's unfair does not change the fact that you have to figure out a solution." Sometimes, however, it's hard to feel anything but rage in these situations. I know that. But stop for a minute and think about it. What good does your anger and rage do? *None!*

A great sentence in an insightful little book by David Maine called *The Preservationist* tells of the Flood story and Noah's reaction: "Through painful experience, he has learned that the net result of raging and railing and cursing and beseeching and boiling is: nothing."

Rage and tears do nothing except make you miserable. Your husband and his girlfriend will go right on doing what they are doing, and no amount of ranting, raving, complaining or crying will change that. I know that's true because I've tried all those negative reactions. All the Radical Women have. They just do not work. *They do not work!* Give them up!

So, you're thinking, "Okay. What can I do? How do I get out of that trap?" Here's a suggestion. It's the only thing any of us have tried that actually does any good. In reality, it makes all the difference in the world. Do this and your life will change. Here's the secret again, repeated for emphasis: *Change your attitude!*

"Research shows pretty clearly that the more people focus on the loss, the more prolonged their grief will be," says George Bonanno, associate professor of clinical psychology at Columbia University, in an article, "Letting go of letting go." Accept your situation. Stop fighting it. Stop obsessing about what's wrong in your life. You don't have to like every single thing about it, but change the way you think about it. The sooner you do that, the better off you'll be.

STOPPING THE MOVIES IN YOUR MIND

For way too long, I produced and directed glorious, full-color, full-length, wide-screen features starring my husband and his girlfriend. I would picture how he touched her, how he kissed her, the things he said to her, where they were, how they laughed.

You will need to develop whatever mind tricks you can to avoid such movies in your mind. Anyone who rebuilds a rich, fulfilling life learns how destructive those mental images are and figures out some way to stop them.

One time I found a blanket and an unrecognized CD of "Romantic Favorites" in the back of my husband's car, and I actually torturously tried to conjure up possible scenarios of the two of them with those stage props. Let me tell you from experience, as you probably know already, that being a movie director with your husband and his lover as romantic co-stars brings nothing but horrible, gut-wrenching, sick-to-your-stomach, unmitigated anguish and pain. Nothing good comes from that. But in the beginning, my mind on its own accord seemed to wander in and around those visions at will.

Keep reminding yourself that these destructive mental images only hurt you. And because they are hurting you, they make things more difficult for those around you whom you care about. Your husband or ex-husband, in the meantime, is still out having a fabulous time on the blanket with his new love in some secluded spot listening to romantic music, and probably having a bottle of wine as well.

I finally decided that to keep my sanity, I had to find a way to stop those images. You can't make room for any new, extraordinary possibilities in your life if your mind is filled with those destructive visions. So, you have to start forcing your mind to focus on something else.

I know that in the beginning especially, it's incredibly hard to focus on any big, grand plans for anything. I tried that. In the very beginning, you have to focus on getting through the next five minutes, then fifteen, then half an hour, then from one hour to the next during the day.

A while back I found something that I had written to myself in my daily planner. It said, "What do I need to do right now for the next three hours to feel better? Then I wrote, "Clean up something!" and drew a rectangle around those words. Next, were the words, "Don't look too far ahead. Right now, just take care of this next hour. It's 9:10. Just get by until 10 o'clock—50 minutes." You have to deal with the increments of time you can handle. It's like dealing with an addiction. One minute at a time. One hour at a time. One day at a time.

Only after you are a ways out of those dark and somber woods can you begin to focus on more than just surviving. Survive first. Then move on to progressively more ambitious visions of the future.

In the meantime, promise yourself that you will figure out some mental image to switch to as soon as ugly pictures show up. If a destructive image comes into your head, promise yourself to *instantly* switch to a positive image. I would often try to focus completely on my children or grandchildren. I would try to visualize what they were doing and then I would pray specifically, in detail, for each one. Sometimes I would automatically visualize my favorite fishing spot in Wyoming. I would envision every detail in my mind—the smell of the pines, the snow-capped mountains, the fish rings appearing out of nowhere in the quiet. Or I would sometimes mentally contemplate my Bible verse for the year. Or meditate on some inspirational thought I had committed to memory.

Do whatever works for you. As soon as a negative image comes into your head, immediately switch to a positive one. *Immediately.* Those negative images do not solve anything or fix anything or make anything better, so as soon as one shows up, replace it with something good.

LIVING IN THE MOMENT

In order to move to acceptance, you must be able to be still within yourself. Accept every single thing about where you are now. Close your eyes and feel peaceful about your situation. For this one minute totally accept where you are now. It is your reality. Don't judge it as good or bad. Don't fight it. A wise friend of mine who is a family therapist said one thing she always tells her patients is, "Do not fight what you inevitably must do." Accept where you are and recognize what you must do. Feel everything that is good about this moment.

You may be saying, "She's got to be kidding! There is nothing good about where I am now!" That's how I felt, too. All of us in the Radical group started at that point. But, I must tell you, there are good things that will come from this. God promises that. Some situations I'll concede take incredible effort and patience. Some life experiences require more faith, trust, and tears than can be imagined. I'm sorry that's true, but in the end, the rewards will outweigh the struggle.

As you begin to learn to live in the present moment, don't concentrate on this hour or this day or this week. Focus on this precise instant. That's the only moment you can do anything about. Don't waste it! Put the past in the past where it belongs, and get your mind as completely as you can into this very precious moment at hand. Where are you right now? Where are you reading this book?

Are you drinking a refreshing glass of ice-cold lemonade? Are you having a steaming, robust cup of coffee out of your favorite mug? (I have several power cups on my shelf.) How does it taste? Do you have on your favorite jeans and sweatshirt? Are you outside in the sun at the beginning of fall with that tiny little nip of coolness just on the edge of the air? Are you on your lunch break at work? Can you hear the cicadas or the birds or the traffic? Are you having a yummy piece of cinnamon bread with the kind of jam you love or a nice crisp apple? Can you smell lilacs or honeysuckle or dinner in the oven? Involve all of your senses in appreciating this one particular moment. Be exquisitely aware of your skin, your sight, your taste, your hearing, your sense of smell. You are alive. You are exactly the person God created you to be, and you have this moment of life to embrace and enjoy.

For now, don't think about the future. For this exercise, be totally aware of only now. Stabilize. Heal. Feel your own inner strength, your creativity, your generosity. Think about the blessing of your children and grandchildren. Be thankful for the measure of health you have. Be thankful for your mind, however crazy it's been lately. Be grateful for, and take delight in, every single good thing in your life at this moment.

After you master the art of thinking about everything that is good about this moment, you can then think about an action that needs to be taken in this moment to improve something in your life. If you aren't happy with your job, you can still, with a spirit of thankfulness about the present, think about what you might need to do to change that circumstance. All happiness and all change begin in this present moment. You can make changes all along the way, if you first perfect the spirit of accepting things just as they are—just for this moment.

Often true happiness has very little to do with possessions or outward circumstances. We don't have to be knocked around by every circumstance of life. We can choose joy regardless of the circumstances. Every day. Every night. Every minute. We have the power to choose joy.

Many years ago, my Mom and I wrote a book called, *Yes, This Day Is for Joy!* The book was written at the request of a hospice organization for terminally ill patients, people who were not going to get better without an outright miracle. It turned out that the book had a much larger audience than we expected and is appropriate for people going through all sorts of life traumas. But what amazes me is that I helped write and illustrate that book. Even though I know those truths in my heart, at the beginning of my own personal catastrophe I wasted so much precious time feeling, not joyful, but despairing, full of rage and defeat.

I've discovered that *telling* someone else about how to be joyful through suffering is easy, but when it's your husband who is making love to another woman, or who wants to leave you and spend the rest of his life with someone else, you forget everything you ever knew about joy. The hurt overcomes us like a tsunami, and we lose our footing temporarily or, for some of us, for several years. I'm sorry to say that some women never fully recover. That's a tragedy.

At the beginning of this journey, there is so much pain and change that it's hard to process it all. We find ourselves reeling, trying to keep from falling on our faces completely, and, after all that talk about savoring the present moment, I realize, too, that the grief and pain must be faced and dealt before you can really feel a sense of joy or gladness about much of anything at all. That's why this topic is where it is.

Each part of this book deals with learning something at a certain level and then, hopefully, moving up to the next rung of healing. We've discussed that joy has to be grabbed in tiny increments wherever and whenever it shows up. It can come from completely enjoying what you are having for lunch, or fully appreciating a nice hot bath or a bowl of perfectly ripe strawberries and real cream or some fresh, warm summer tomatoes. It comes from being exquisitely aware of the magnificence of your surroundings whatever they are.

This progression of getting better follows Maslow's famous Hierarchy of Needs, first published in 1943. Reviewing this landmark list—which you may have learned in school— will help you see where you are in the recovery process.

The original list had five levels of needs. First, Physiological Needs—the need for enough air, food, water and rest in order to survive. Second, Safety Needs—the need for shelter and clothing and protection from life-threatening forces. Third, Social Needs—the desire to be accepted, appreciated or loved by others. Fourth, Self-Esteem Needs—the desire to respect ourselves and to be respected by others. Fifth, Self-Actualization Needs—the need to fulfill our potential, to become everything we are capable of being.

Maslow's concept is that each level builds on the ones before to bring us to ever-higher planes of self-fulfillment. In reality, the needs listed are constantly being met and fulfilled at different times—and sometimes all at once. However, it is true that we can't address the need for personal fulfillment if we don't have enough food to eat or water to drink or air to breathe. It's hard for a woman to reach a level of increased self-esteem if her house is being taken away or her safety isn't assured. So take your time and deal with each stage as it comes. When you're ready, move on.

After figuring out how to deal with the earliest stages of meeting the basic needs of sustenance and sleep, the Radical Women started tackling the higher levels of what we needed. Some of us fluctuated back and forth even after we had learned the lessons of the previous levels. This is not a smooth progression of crossing certain skills off the list, then effortlessly moving on. It is easy to talk about "This Day is for Joy," but when I tried to live it out in my situation, I struggled and slogged through every day and every level just like everyone else.

DECIDING TO MOVE ON

Finally one day, from somewhere deep in my brain, I realized—"I think I've done just about all the slogging I want to do." I had felt every minute of the pain and suffering of this situation, and one day, I finally said, "I've had enough pain. More suffering is not going to move me to any place good. More anger and worry and sadness is not going to get me to the place I want to be." I don't remember the exact date, and I still regress to my old ways occasionally, but I do remember coming to the conclusion that "I'm ready to move on." I even wrote in my journal, "I'm done with all of this ridiculous sobbing."

I finally consciously made the decision, "I am going to take where I am at this very moment and appreciate it, be thankful I've survived this far, and start making the rest of my life the very best it can be." And remember, our happiness does not depend on our marital status. The Apostle Paul, in 1 Corinthians, says, "Don't be wishing you were someplace else or with someone else. Where you are right now is God's place for you. Live and obey and love and believe right there. God, not your marital status, defines your life."

Happiness does not depend on how much money we have or where we live. It depends on how well we can learn to embrace God and the myriad of good things that are available in this present moment.

Here are a few things to think about in looking at what is happening in this precise moment. If you aren't doing these things, right now, why not?

THE RIGHT NOW CHECKLIST

Are you using your potential?

Are you doing something that brings you joy?

Are you helping someone else?

Are you doing some small thing to make the world a better place?

Are you enjoying the physical sensations of the moment?

Are you doing something that is worthwhile?

Are you making a situation easier for someone else?

Are you thankful for something?

Are you using your talents?

Are you using your God-given gifts to bring your unique light to the world?

If you want to be doing something different than what you are doing at this moment, take a physical action that will bring a desired reality into your life.

When our present moments are totally filled doing something we want to be doing or that brings good to our life—taking a class, creating something beautiful or useful, cooking a meal, enjoying a book, playing the piano, taking a walk, playing chess, solving a problem at work, cleaning the basement, de-cluttering your house, taking care of a grandchild—and when we are totally immersed in the present moment doing something valuable or pleasurable, we suddenly find that happiness has found us on its own. Cherish those moments. Lose yourself. Concentrate completely on and appreciate exactly what you are doing at this moment.

"when we are totally immersed in the present moment doing something valuable or pleasurable, we suddenly find that happiness has found us on its own. Cherish those moments."

Get involved in things that actually interest you. If you are interested in art, go to an art opening. And don't be afraid to go by yourself. Tag along with a couple if you want to and then branch out on your own. Volunteer at a community food kitchen or at Habitat for Humanity. We feel better when we help someone else. "It's better to give than to receive" has become a cliche, but it is absolutely true. God has been trying to tell us that all along.

You may be alone. Your kids may be married or in college. Your husband is definitely gone. Instead of feeling sorry for yourself, take this time to give yourself away in brand new ways. Offer to give a shower for a friend's child who is getting married. Have a campout at your house with your grandchildren.

For one week each summer, one Radical friend who lived in the country had "Mimi's Camp" with her grandchildren. I actually have two friends who do "Mimi's Camp." My Radical Mimi planned fun activities on a theme like "Music and Art" or "Indians and Pioneers." By sharing her talents and her joy about life, she created fantastic memories for her grandchildren—and for herself. I'll guarantee that while you are entertaining seven or eight grandchildren for the weekend you won't have time to be depressed, and they will cherish those times forever.

Take your grandchild or a neighbor's child or your niece or nephew on a weekend trip, or spend the night at a hotel close by. Get some sleeping bags and sleep with your grandchildren on your screened-in porch or in the backyard under the stars. While you have time, give yourself to a worthwhile charity or a good cause. Help in the nursery at church. Give yourself away in any way that makes you feel good.

While you're at it, set aside some time to just admire and appreciate nature—even if you're not a nature girl. I remember clearly the first year that I went to Wyoming with my family after my husband and I separated. My family members have gone there for a week each summer for 34 years. The weather that trip was unusually cold, but I found that just being out in the freezing rain was good for me. My hands were often red with cold, and sometimes I could hardly tie on a new fly to fish with, but I was completely absorbed in the moment. The physical discomfort of the chilling rain was nothing compared to the emotional agony I had been experiencing, and, in fact, it was a nice change of pace in a weird sort of way.

Early on, however, almost all of nature made me sad in one way or another. The beauty of the dawn made me sad. A rainstorm punctuated by deep, rich thunder made me sad. A bright sunny day made me sad. The moon always made me sad. There is no getting around all that in the beginning. Feel that grief as long as you must, then move on and recognize anew the refreshment available in the majesty of nature all around you. See nature's glory for the glory itself.

I wrote the thoughts below as I tried to get myself into the moment one beautiful spring evening. I was by myself. Our youngest was still away at college, and after dinner I sat on the front porch in my quiet comfortable neighborhood.

May Fourth - As God Designed It

Birds ... calming in the twilight
Leaves ... still with quiet contentment
Air ... a lilac-sweet profusion
Red and pink tulips ... standing boldly
Everything being perfectly what it is.
No wanting to be something else.
No desiring to be somewhere else.
No wishing things were different.
Just being ...
> *and growing ...*
>> *and knowing at this very moment,*
>>> *everything is happening just as it should.*

Focus on all of your blessings. Focus on the lessons you are learning that will bring more goodness and pure simple pleasure into your life. Think about how to make every moment in your life the bright shining pleasure it can be. This moment, and every moment, can be good or bad. Only you can decide.

CHAPTER EIGHT

EMBRACE TRANSFORMATION

Radical means 'seeking to make drastic reforms.' Each one of us decides what those reforms will look like. We can turn into promoters of 'poor me' or we can be the amazing women God created us to be. It's our call.

About Him

I hate him
I hate who he is
I hate his arrogance
I hate his selfishness
I hate what he did to this family
I hate how he misleads everyone to make himself look good
I hate how he pretends to be this wonderful caring person
I wish he were dead
My life would be easier if he were dead
Our children's lives would be easier if he were dead
He's narcissistic
Every single thing is about him
He's superficial ... there's no vulnerability
He is a self-absorbed person
He doesn't listen
He drinks too much
He lies to my face
He sneaks off and sleeps with a woman who is not his wife
He does not love his children ... he says he does but he wouldn't do this if
he did
He does not love me ... he says he does but he really only loves himself
He does not love his little mistress on the side ... he says he does but he uses
her for his pleasure and ego
He thinks he is Mr. Cool, Mr. Desirable
What he really is, is pathetic. His actions are self-serving and despicable
He is not a real man—he is a coward.
He acts so concerned about everyone
but he cares mostly about how he looks to all of his "admirers"
I hate him
Except for our children and grandchildren,
*   I hate the relationship I had with him*

I hate the time I spent trying to please him ...
> *trying to build a real relationship*
He has no clue about real relationships, real life
He is absolutely incapable of seeing the big picture
He doesn't get it. He will never get it.
I want to be free from his influence
I want to never see him again
I want him DEAD! DEAD! DEAD!

I shudder to admit it. I wrote those words. I had hate in my heart. I actually wished a person dead that I had been married to for 33 years. I actually wished at that moment that the father of my children were dead. Even though those words, true or not, were exactly what I was feeling, they were not loving. They were not compassionate, forgiving nor gentle. They were words of rage, hurt and earth-shaking, heart-breaking disappointment.

When I look back at where I was emotionally, spiritually and even physically when I wrote those words, and then see where I am today, I'm amazed at the transformation. I went from an utterly heartbroken, despairing condition to bitterness and rage and finally to a place of joy, hope and happiness. What happened?

This whole book deals with the insights the Radical Women uncovered to get to the good side of this experience. Our first step was to decide to survive and rise above it. To do that, we all kept plugging along, inching along, day after day. Some days, we did all right. Some days we floundered. Some days we blew it, and had to go back a step and start again. We hope our experiences will make your trip a little easier.

The real story is about the transformation. The God part. The Radical part. The part that makes the life-changing difference. Each of the Radical Women can tell about what was learned, but eventually you have to learn the lessons yourself. And the lessons are not easy. I still slip back at times, and forget God's purposes for me. But I believe now more than ever that God is the transcendent answer to every life question. He is the transcendent solution to

> *"I always rebelled when I heard those words, 'It just takes time. This will get better with time.' In the beginning I thought to myself, "I will never get over this. This will never get better."*

every life problem. He is the transcendent bread of life for every hunger we will ever have.

The transformation process took the Radical Women through these steps: Grieving, Dealing with the Big Questions, Struggling to Forgive, Surrendering, and finally, Choosing Transformation.

GRIEVING

Soon after the divorce was final, I was seeing a counselor who said, "You can usually count on about one year for every five to seven years of marriage before you really get this behind you."

I said, "I don't accept that! I'm not going to spend six or seven years getting over this!" Well, it did not take me six or seven years, but it did take longer that I wanted it to. Grieving takes time. Recovery takes time. I always rebelled when I heard those words, "It just takes time. This will get better with time."

In the beginning I thought to myself, "I will never get over this. This will never get better. I will feel like this for the rest of my life," and I meant it. I thought I would grieve, at least privately, until I died. But when I started actually trying to get over it and move on, I thought I might not physically survive six or seven years of feeling like I did.

Grieving was new to me. I have never lost a parent, a sibling, a child, even a close friend. So, the sick-in-my-heart, sick-to-my-stomach, deep sighing kind of pain I was feeling was something I had never experienced. The oppression covers everything you do and everything you experience with a muffling, gray all-enclosing sadness. Every breath and every move takes effort. You stare at the ceiling at night. As hard as you try to "pull yourself out of it," you fail.

Grief is a process that can't be sidestepped or hurried. Accept that you have to grieve, and grieve deeply, the loss of your husband and your marriage and everything they meant to you.

The Radical Women went through the steps in this book in order to get better. All those steps moved us forward, and in the end, the minutes and the hours and the days and the months added up to enough time, and most of us finally turned the corner.

Grief has a life of its own that must be endured, survived and finally somehow assimilated into a new life. It's an agonizing journey. But grief can also be a valley from which we can glimpse the majestic mountain of God. This physical and emotional struggle forces us to consider what God has been offering all along—a way to transcend our suffering.

We are driven by grief to ask the big questions: Who am I? Why am I on this earth? What am I supposed to be doing? From this darkness of grief comes the realization that our life on earth is just part of the equation. An inkling inside says, "I'm more than this body. My experiences on this earth are more than just my daily comings and goings. There is something bigger than I am out there. There is some purpose for me being here."

Dealing with the Big Questions

My long, painful journey through grief was very distressing to me because I am a Christian. I was a Christian all through this. I didn't think a "real" Christian would suffer emotionally like I was suffering. I had felt God in my life before, but I thought a "real" Christian would not be so discouraged and hopeless, and would accept God's will and move on. I wanted answers, and maybe the questions were harder for me to ask, because I already had a relationship with God.

I knew that God doesn't automatically make his children's lives a never-ending trip to a cosmic amusement park, but how could God have allowed this to happen when I was trying my best to serve him? I wanted God to show me what good he possibly had in mind through the destruction of our family. And I continued hoping until the end of the marriage that God might bring a last-minute miracle that would fix everything.

During those desperate days, when I felt like a spiritual failure and wondered where God was, I still reached out for God, prayed to God, cried to God, complained to God and fell on my face before God. He was my last hope, and at the time, he just didn't seem to be doing anything to help. There were no answers at all that I could see.

In looking back, the truth is, he was fixing everything even though I didn't realize it. He was acting all along, and he continues to bring miracles even now. But in the beginning, I was so steeped in sorrow, I couldn't see his miracles, because they definitely were not the miracles I asked for, nor the miracles I expected.

When we start asking those big questions about life and about God, we most likely won't see definite answers at first, but we can start to see the Radical transcendent possibilities of our existence.

I believe the Bible and its affirmations that there is a God, that he wants a relationship with me, that he has provided a way for me to establish and develop that relationship, and that he can and will live in and through me if I let him. When you think about those statements, they in themselves are about as Radical as you can get.

I also believe the New Testament account that God became a man through Jesus Christ, who came to earth as a human being to help me understand his love and to demonstrate how to be the whole, full, complete person we are each intended to be. I believe that, still.

No one has all the answers, but I do know that in my life, and especially through this experience, the God I have been trying to know and serve has become more real and more personal than ever.

Early on I took that hesitant "leap of faith" to believe that the Bible is God's inspired revelation of himself to us, and that he has given us this guidebook to help us make daily decisions about how best to live on this earth. I am not an expert in the canon. I have not studied how we got every book and how best to understand every word written there, but I do know the principles found in the New Testament are definitely Radical. And from my own experience, I know the day-to-day practice of those principles can bring a life of joy and peace and incredible fulfillment to anyone who really lives out what those principles teach. It is in the New Testament that we are introduced to the Holy Spirit who is God himself, embodied as an entity who comes and lives within this conglomeration of atoms that is me. It's revolutionary! It's remarkable! And it's real!

This Radical thought of God in us takes us beyond just following the rules. It's an intimate relationship with God himself who shows us that the things on this earth are just shadows of the world of the spirit.

I wrote this during the time when I was trying to come to grips with where I was and where I longed to be:

Spirit World/Earth World
Sometimes I feel like my soul exists in the God-world ...
  the world of light and truth and joy and contentment
While my body exists in the Earth-world of pain and disappointment
  the world of broken dreams and unkept promises,
  betrayals, endless tears and constant struggle.
My earth body sees my children ache because of lies and lost security
  and disappointed trust.
I must teach them that the God-world is the real world ...
  and our truest selves can always celebrate the abundance
  of Spirit living
And that even though our bodies moan with the agony of deepest hurts
  and the pain of being strangers in a foreign land
Our spirits can still soar.
I must teach them that in spite of human disappointments,
  the Spirit will prevail
  and will cover us with a soft, sure joy
  and a quiet, unshakeable, tangible peace.

God promises that if we believe that he is, and that he sent his son to make us right with him, he will move us out of the earth-world into the spirit-world. We are living in this fallen world where there is suffering and sadness on every side. The day-to-day living on this earth is not always easy. God knows that, and he wants us to realize that he can transform our everyday struggles into opportunities to know him better. He also wants to transform us into his messengers of light and hope. God invites us into that relationship with himself and with others. The only trouble is, he often seems to send the invitation through suffering.

In looking back to where I was in the beginning of this experience, I know God's Spirit was moving in my life and was teaching me things that I couldn't learn any other way except through grief and suffering. I felt alone. God wanted me to recognize that he is my constant companion. I felt weak. God was teaching me that his greatest power is shown through weakness. I felt abandoned and lonely and afraid. God was telling me that he is all I need. I knew I was sinful, because of the ugly things I was feeling. God reassured me that I don't have to be perfect because he is my perfect salvation.

One of the core building blocks to transcendent living is that God promises throughout scripture that we will find him if we seek him with all of our heart. An unwanted midlife divorce will make you do that. That's not comfortable, but it's good, nonetheless.

Grief makes you search for answers. Pain makes you search deeply and desperately. Suffering makes you try to figure out if there is a God, and if so, what kind of God he is to allow this. You wonder if he even knows or cares what is happening in your life. The answers don't come overnight. Just keep searching. You will find him. Don't give up. He loves you already. He is already working on your behalf, and he will be beside you every step of the way giving you his power to help you overcome this and bring you to an infinitely better place. A place you probably can't even picture right now.

Struggling to Forgive

Throughout the divorce I longed to believe that good would win, justice would prevail, and truth would be victorious in the end. I wanted reassurance about that, because from my point of view nothing was fair about this situation.

In the beginning I was determined to make things come out right, even if I had to do it myself! God wanted me to look at the situation in a different way. Opposite the "hate" poem at the first of this chapter, I later wrote:

What does God WANT me to think?

God says ...
Don't hate him.
Love him. Forgive him. Be kind. Be patient.
God says ... Revenge is my job. Not yours.
I will deal with him. You can't.
I will make sure justice is done.
I will let him reap what he has sown.
God says, I am not fooled. Trust me.
He may fool everyone else, but he does not fool me.
I see him for who he is.
I see how he treats those I have given him.
I see how he hurts those I have entrusted to his care.
I will hold him accountable for what he does, not what he says.
He and everyone else will someday see who he really is.
Everyone will know. There will be no hiding.
That day will come.
For everyone.
For YOU, too.
So you must free yourself from the negative emotions of hate and anger and bitterness.
Fill yourself with light, joy, peace, love, goodness, laughter.
I will take care of everything.

Don't look at the surface.
Don't worry about how things seem.
*You just accept all of my promises of joy and abundance for **your** life.*
*You let all the good things I promise become the reality of **your** life.*
I have wonderful, amazing things planned for you.
I will give you everything you need.
I will give you the desires of your heart.
Believe me. Trust me. Obey me.
I will take care of everything.

While the first poem was written with fury and disgust, the second and quieter poem was more reflective. I wanted to know how God wanted me, as his follower, to think about this man who had hurt me and our children and had upended every single thing in my life, and was still affecting my life in a negative way. I knew God wanted me to stand up for righteousness and hold my husband accountable for his continued adultery, but I also knew that I was not doing very well demonstrating God's love.

I knew that I was not trusting God to take care of this. I wanted vengeance myself. My human inclination was to make my husband realize the suffering he had caused, and in doing so, get some sort of cosmic compensation for the pain he had created for so many people. I wanted him to spend a few hundred agonizing days and dozens of sleepless nights like I had spent. I wanted him to be sorry, or at the very least, to understand some little inkling of what he had done. Yet God continually tried to get across to me that a peaceful heart, a generous attitude, and a forgiving spirit are best not only for God's purposes, but for me as well.

Most of the Radical Women had real trouble with the whole issue of forgiveness. Most of us could have forgiven our husbands for their affairs if they had been remorseful, stopped their other relationships and asked us for forgiveness. But none of the husbands did. Most of us would have willingly gone to counseling and addressed our problems, but we found that impossible while our husbands were actively involved with other women—and often lying about it.

My husband would never stop seeing his girlfriend, even while we were in counseling. He would promise to; he would tell me he had; but he never actually ended that emotional and physical relationship with her until we were divorced more than three years later. So I really did not know how to forgive a continuing betrayal, and one he would not take responsibility for. The other Radical Women felt the same way.

Christ himself in the Gospel of Matthew says that God forgives me with the same forgiveness I forgive others. Considering the unforgiveness that was in my heart about my husband's continued infidelity, that was a terrifying thought! I did not feel compassionate at all. I felt both furious and broken-hearted. Yet, God commands—yes commands—us to be forgiving and loving no matter what.

Through it all, God was telling me to stop worrying about my ex-husband getting what he deserved and do things instead that assured that I get what I deserve. He told me to stop worrying that there were no just consequences, and instead to take control of my own actions and stop trying to change someone else's. God told me what would work, and work every time—without fail. *Love.* Now that's truly Radical.

Love transforms us. Love chooses to accept another person as a fellow struggler, a fellow traveler. That does not mean accepting abusive behavior or being a doormat. That does not mean standing by while your husband breaks his marriage vows again and again. Love means defending God's way of life ... with gentleness. Love means practicing forgiveness and a generosity of heart that comes from God himself.

As the affair continued for those three years, my heart grew less generous about both my husband and the woman he was involved with. Later my attitude toward her changed.

I have an office in my home, and one warm summer day after our divorce, she showed up at my door wearing shorts and a t-shirt, obviously distressed.

She said she was worried about my ex-husband. She said, "He won't answer my phone calls. I'm afraid he might do something dumb ... something to hurt himself. I thought you might know where he is." She continued with real anxiety in her voice, "I think he might be seeing someone else. He told me he was going to be on call, and I found out he wasn't on call. I just can't trust him. How can you have a relationship with someone you can't trust?" She asked this with tears in her eyes.

At first, I couldn't believe this was happening. I could not believe she was telling me these things. She and my husband had betrayed me, yet here she was sitting on a stool in my kitchen. She had divorced *her* husband. She was living in an apartment waiting for *my* ex-husband, and he was not answering her calls.

At that moment, I looked at her and thought, "What a sad, pathetic woman. What a painful life she has made for herself." That was the beginning. I began to let my hatred toward her go, and began to feel pity instead.

Forgiveness is a complex topic. I've read books and articles about it. I've talked to my family and my counselor about it—and to the Radical Women. So many questions emerge, and they are real and important questions: Have you really forgiven if you are still angry? Can you forgive someone if they are not sorry? Can you forgive someone if they never stop their destructive behavior? Can you ever forget the hurt? Is forgetting even possible—or necessary? What about unforgiving thoughts that creep into our minds years later? What about the new hurts that emerge?

These questions encompass tough theological issues, and I can't answer them for anyone but myself. I finally got to some level of forgiveness and peace in my heart, by saying to God, "I can't do this on my own. I'm not even sure what forgiveness is. All I know is I want to be forgiving because you desire it ... you command it, and I want to move on. Help me do what I need to do to let this go. *I need your help!* Show me what to do!"

Forgiveness seems to be a gift and an act of the will. I want to be free from the negativity of unforgiveness. By holding onto unforgiving feelings, our life does not have a chance at being what we want it to be. An unforgiving spirit breeds anxiety, tension, anger and bitterness. All of those ugly emotions make it impossible to move on to the good life God wants to give us, and I definitely wanted to move on.

I wanted to follow God's direction for my life, so I first asked God's forgiveness for my own wrongdoings in every area of my life. I had already written my ex-husband asking for his forgiveness for anything I had done that made him feel unloved or hurt. I forgave him in writing for everything he had done, including his affairs.

After a lesson on reconciliation one Sunday in which the preacher seemed to be talking directly to me, I called the woman my ex-husband was involved with and told her I held no hard feelings for her. I didn't say, "I forgive you," because I didn't want to sound holier than thou. She thought I had an ulterior motive, and was not very receptive. But I did my part the best I could.

Early on, I worried that the residual anger and hurt I felt meant that I hadn't forgiven. I came to believe, though, that if you truly want to be forgiving, and do your best to be forgiving, that's all you can do at any given moment.

I think everyone has to go through stages before a true sense of forgiveness is reached. It seems, too, that forgiveness doesn't mean you will never be angry toward or hurt by that person again. Forgiveness is realizing that we are all human, we all make mistakes, yet God has forgiven all of us for our many shortcomings, and we are commanded to do the same.

All I know is that I was tired of the whole thing, and God seemed to be saying that forgiveness was the key to the release I needed. Finally I said, "Okay, God, I've tried to do what you asked. I've done the best I can right now with the forgiveness thing. I don't understand it completely, but you said this is what you want me to do, so I've done it."

SURRENDERING

To some of the Radical Women, surrender meant surrendering to the situation as it was. An acceptance—a coming to grips with the reality of it and making some sort of peace.

For me, the surrender was to God. I said out loud in my kitchen, "God, I have decided to really go out on a limb here and give myself and my future totally to you to do with as you will." It was not an easy or pretty surrender. I did not have a warm cloud of truth shimmering around me. The reality was, I had tried almost everything else, and it was as if to say, "Okay! All right! I give up!"

Every morning for awhile, I would specifically verbalize something like this: "Hey, God, it's me. I have no idea what you have planned for me today, but whatever it is I will try to do the best I can to follow your will with joy. P.S. It would help a lot if you would make yourself more clear."

I asked God to "bring me the people you want me to touch. Give me the words you want me to say. Work in my business with my clients. Help me help them accomplish what they want to accomplish, and let me shine your light while I do that. Help me lead my children and grandchildren to see you today. Help them be assured when they look at my life that you are real and that your way of life works. Forgive me when I have not shown that to all of the people around me. Use me God. I'm weak and sinful and full of faults, but in the Bible you used all kinds of weak and sinful men and women. The harlot who helped the Israelite spies. Peter who denied Christ. Paul who tortured Christians. You used all of those sinful, weak people to do your work. Use me. I will try to get out of the way."

Occasionally, after offering my weak, somewhat pitiful, somewhat hopeful self to God, I would stand by the window for a few minutes and try to feel his love and power working in and around and through me. Sometimes I could feel it. Sometimes I couldn't. But at least I felt like I was giving God a real chance in my life. I definitely had a growing confidence of being where God wanted me to be. For a change I felt excited about what the day would bring, and I had a growing positive anticipation about the future.

When I got to that point of (somewhat reluctant) submission and conscious release, God went into high gear. Although I was brought up in a deeply committed Christian home, and I knew of God's unbelievable grace and love for me, I didn't fully appreciate or understand God's continual acting on my behalf.

I have always been grateful for his amazing gifts to me. He gave his only Son for me. He redeemed me for his own. He knows my name and every single thing about me. He loves me enough to make a plan to bring me to his side. He gives me a way to conquer death and live a glorious life forever, beginning right now. I have known those things on a certain level most of my life, but not on the "utterly amazed that he loves me this much" gut-level way that I know them now.

Before the affair, my life seemed to be going great most of the time. My family was good. My problems were minor. I prayed daily. I read the Word of God expectantly and with a desire to live by the principles I found there. I was trying to live how God wanted me to live. Everyone was healthy and happy. We usually had enough money, even though our credit card balances were too high. I desired God's presence. Then, however, I didn't really recognize either the depth of my need for God nor how he truly loves and cares for me.

This experience made me realize without a doubt that I desperately need divine help. I don't want some human band-aid. I don't want some mantra-chanting or positive-thinking guru or even Dr. Phil. I want a Radical, religious-platitude-shattering life change! I realized once-and-for-all that I don't have a chance without God.

The realization of my total dependence on God is responsible for the dramatic change in my life. I don't want God on the periphery. I want to be directed by him every single minute of every single day and to feel his love covering me completely. That's all.

At first, at the beginning of this storm, I thought *I* had to fix everything. I tried to fix myself. I felt responsible to fix this situation for my children. I tried to fix my finances. I tried to fix my social life. I tried to fix the holidays and family get-togethers. I tried to fix the faucet in the bathroom. I know that we all need to do our part to make a bad situation better. We need to depend on friends and family and our own power and will to make the best of a situation, but in the end, after we do everything we can, we must realize that we can't possibly fix it all. All we can do is the best we can at any given moment, and then stop worrying and give the results to God.

When I finally realized that I mainly needed to fix myself and get myself where I should be, the rest of these things started working themselves out.

I discovered that most of the time the best thing I could do was take a deep breath and do something positive. Something good. Even something fun. Take cookies to a neighbor. Give a huge tip to the sacker at the grocery store. Go see my granddaughter dance or my grandson play basketball. I'm convinced God doesn't want me struggling, agonizing through every day. He wants me to know that he is in control, and remember that he is with me—every step of the way.

My divorce was the first time my faith had been put to the test in such a defining way. Christian clichés are easy when everyone is nice, you have enough of everything, your family is doing fine and your life is humming along. But it's not so easy when you are asked to practice God's principles in the face of the suffering and utter sadness and a sense of abandonment. I wanted a Radical change. I was tired to death of feeling worried, sad, lonely, angry and defeated. I wanted to remember what it was like to put my head back and really laugh at something. Anything.

In the beginning I was often mad at God because it seemed as if he wasn't doing anything. I wanted a burning bush! Writing on the wall! My enemies struck dead in their tracks! I wanted God to show his stuff! The fact is, God has been answering my prayers all along—but in ways I never could have imagined. In his own perfect time, he took what I thought I wanted and gave me what I really needed after making sure I learned the lessons he wanted me to learn. I am not a patient person. That was, and still is, part of the problem. I'm continually learning. As Psalms says, "Be still and know that I am God."

Getting through this process of recovery is not easy. The challenges of financial difficulties, new social relationships, family changes—none of those things are easy. But God is working even when we can't see it. He was working even when I was in my bed at night filled with loneliness and despair. He was there even when I was impatient and furious and fretful and worried. God was working through all of that to bring me to a place where I finally understand that life on earth is completely precarious and unpredictable, but at the same time, it's surrounded by and indwelt by and protected by the most powerful, constant, loving reality of the universe.

That reality we call God is continually working on my behalf, and he will use challenges to refine me into the person he created me to be. God can turn even complainers, whiners and worriers like me into bold, loyal, courageous wonder women. God will help us show the world that whatever the outward circumstances, love is the best course every time. By making the decision to let God's love shine through us, we can't, ultimately, be defeated. By disasters. By cancer. By successes and victories. By heartbreak. By the actions of anyone else.

> *"With God, we have the power to be victorious no matter what, because we already know how the story ends, and we always have the choice to love."*

With God, we have the power to be victorious no matter what, because we already know how the story ends, and we always have the choice to love.

Let me warn you, though, as any Radical person can attest, once you say, "Okay God, I'm yours," he will take you at your word, and you will have no idea what kind of wild ride will be in store. We become part of God's great master plan, but none of us, at that point, can know how he will use us.

When I found myself in this lonely life situation, I know I said, "Wait a minute! I don't like this play! I don't want this part! I just want a comfy happy life!" I didn't realize God was trying to use my circumstances to create a new—and better—life for me, and I fought every step of the way. We often want to stay in our lounge chair of low expectations, when God wants to take us on a fantastic and glorious adventure!

A Brother's Letter About Victimhood

Dear sis:

Quit worrying that people will think [your ex-husband] had every reason to find someone else. No one who knows anything about this thinks that. Even if you were the worst wife in the world (which you weren't), he still did wrong. What he did was wrong no matter how you look at it. His actions were still sinful and demonstrated a lack of character and integrity. He did great harm not only to you, but to his children, his family, your family, your friends, his group, his lover, her husband, her children, her family, her career. He left destruction all over the place and everyone knows that.

But even so, that's not your fault. He made those choices himself. All you need to worry about is being responsible for living as much like God wants you to as possible. All you have to do is accept responsibility for your own actions this minute ... right now.

I've shed tears over you about your hurt and sadness, but you have to be mature enough to believe what God says. Let this situation go. Right now ... Let it go! Grab life by the throat and live it as close to God as you can. Have fun! Be joyful! Be happy! Be strong! Be bold! (Even if you don't like being by yourself at the swim team parties.) You have God and all of his power in your life. He has promised you everything good and full and abundant if you just trust him and live according to his principles.

Quit acting like a victim! God's children are never victims! John the Baptist wasn't a victim. Paul wasn't a victim. Stephen wasn't a victim! Joseph wasn't a victim! Christ was not a victim! You are not a victim! ...

So quit saying, "Poor me!" "Poor, pitiful me! Poor kids!" Just believe God.

Remember, we're not victims ... we're conquerors!

Your brother, (W)

BEING TRANSFORMED

God, his Son and his Spirit take our lives—even in our reluctance and fear and insecurity. As the Gospel of Luke says, "We're going to give you a life you won't believe! A life with more blessings than you can hold!" God has promised you joy, peace and love overflowing; you know your eternal future is secure and it's already started, but you have a job to do in the here and now.

What an amazing, Radical, transcendent truth! God has something specific and personally fulfilling planned for each one of us. God has patiently been bringing me to the point of accepting that he really is in control. He guarantees, if I will only let him, that he will make my life an exquisite journey of both serenity and surprise.

Paul wrote to the Galatians, "But what happens when we live God's way? He brings gifts into our lives, much the same way that fruit appears in an orchard ... things like affection for others, exuberance about life and serenity." I want those things. He promises his presence. His care. His blessings. He brings comfort in hundreds of ways. Our children and grandchildren. Friends. Family. Authors. Songs. Art. Sermons. Nature. His Word. Laughter. His Spirit.

Don't settle for a mediocre life. Don't think you're going to just have to "make do" because of your new life circumstances. See what God wants to do with you! Let him use you and use this situation! Be open to his working. God is calling us right now, even in the middle of this mid-life awakening, to a more energetic, more vigorous, more radiant life than we can even imagine. God tells us over and over and over again, "Don't be afraid. Don't be afraid. Don't be afraid." Bravely step up and live with fresh energy and confidence every single day.

To get us where he wants us, God is continually teaching us the Radical concept of accepting every circumstance of life as a gift. Paul says in 2 Corinthians, "Isn't it wonderful all the ways in which this distress has goaded you closer to God? You're more alive, more concerned, more sensitive, more reverent, more human, more passionate, more responsible." Let this new life happen! Walk confidently in God!

God says to us, while I'm working this situation out, here's what I want you to do. You love me and love your neighbor. That's it in a nutshell. Be joyful. Be at peace. Trust me to work out the details. Act as if your life is unfolding just as it should. (It is!) Live in unshakeable gratitude for what I am doing. (I am working things out for your best!) Remember, I am in control. I am bringing you blessings even through this. Stop worrying about yourself and start showing your love for me by loving others. Love begets love. What goes around, comes around. I am the author of that reality. You will reap what you sow. If you sow sin and selfishness and ignore me, you will reap a life that is dead, empty, and dull. If you sow real love, your life will be a bouquet of beauty so exquisite you can't even describe it.

> *"God says to us, while I'm working this situation out, here's what I want you to do. You love me and love your neighbor. That's it in a nutshell."*

"Okay," you say, "I sowed love in my marriage. I tried to be what I needed to be and look what it got me. Anguish and pain." God knows that. Be patient. God never lets the good things we do or the bad things we go through be wasted. Paul says it like this in his letter to the early Christians, "Throw yourselves into the work of the Master, confident that nothing you do for him is a waste of time or effort." God sees and rewards every single good thing we do. Maybe not at the moment. Maybe not when we think we should be rewarded, but he sees every cup of water we give to a thirsty fellow traveler, every encouragement we gave our husband.

God through Paul says in his Letter to the Galatians, "Don't be misled: No one makes a fool of God. What a person plants, he will harvest. The person who plants selfishness, ignoring the needs of others—ignoring God!—harvests a crop of weeds. All he'll have to show for his life is weeds! But the one who plants in response to God, letting God's Spirit do the growth work in him, harvests a crop of real life, eternal life. So let's not allow ourselves to get fatigued doing good. At the right time we will harvest a good crop if we don't give up."

King David talks of his life transformation this way in the Psalms:

> "But me he (God) caught—reached all the way
> > from sky to sea; he pulled me out
> of that ocean of hate, that enemy chaos,
> the void in which I was drowning ...
> GOD made my life complete
> > when I placed all the pieces before him.
> When I got my act together
> > he gave me a fresh start.
> Now I'm alert to GOD's ways;
> > I don't take GOD for granted.
> Every day I review the ways he works,
> > I try not to miss a trick
> I feel put back together
> > and I'm watching my step.
> GOD rewrote the text of my life
> > when I opened the book of my heart to his eyes.

Because God is in control, we are never victims of a person or a circumstance. We become God's ambassador, God's emissary, God's beacon of hope and light for hurting people—in our homes, in the operating room, in the classroom, at the homeless shelter, at the art gallery, in the courtroom, at the home for abused children, at parties, in prison, in the boardroom, in the inner city, in the suburbs. Wherever God puts us, he beams his light.

The people in your life will see your courage and appreciate your determination to do right whatever the situation, and they will be inspired to do the same. Your children need to see this. Your friends and neighbors need to see this. Your coworkers need to see this. Let them all see God's bold confidence instead of worry. Let them see God's strength instead of fear. Let them see God's expansive provision instead of the poverty of a small and anxious life. Let them see God's bright, irrepressible love in everything you do! Life is meant to be celebrated—that includes your life, especially now. Because of our actions, people are reassured that with God they can conquer the hurts in their own lives. They see by your life that transformation brings rewards on a completely new level.

I'm sorry people didn't see more of that reality in me during the early stages of my divorce. I wasted a lot of precious time and effort crying, worrying and complaining, not to mention all the screaming and shouting I did.

In writing this, I've worried that it sounds too revolutionary. Too far out. Too far-fetched. I know these ideas are Radical. Radical doesn't just mean "rising above divorce in confidence and love." It means facing every situation in life with God's promise that he can transform it into something amazingly good for us and for those around us. This isn't a "wade in the water" of surface spirituality. This isn't divining crystals, "going to church," or putting on the outward appearance of being religious. This is a no-turning-back free fall into the big, wide universe of God.

God says if we give everything to him, he will do the rest. He says, "Try my Radical way of living this adventure, and I promise that you will discover truths that will revolutionize absolutely everything. Your life in me will be beyond your wildest dreams!"

EPILOGUE

REFLECTIONS ON MY LIFE NOW

I am thankful for my ex-husband for many reasons, but mainly because of our four children and the seven—so far—grandchildren we share. His genes are part of who they are, and I love them all more than I could ever say. I am proud of the truly amazing people they have turned out to be. I know I am their mother and grandmother, but they really are amazing! We also have been blessed with incredible daughters-in-law.

God watched over our family in so many ways during our 33 years of marriage. Our children developed into strong, healthy, good people with talents on every side, and I appreciate every single thing my ex-husband did to make that happen. Our children learned many valuable things from him and valuable things from me, too, through all those years. We had lots of fun, memorable, cherished times together. We still have strong, supportive extended families and wonderful friends. Many good things came out of our life together for 33-plus years, and I am thankful for all of them.

It's a great blessing to have a good, primary family that lasts forever. That's how God planned for families to be. However, as you know, that's not always how it works out, even after our very best efforts and countless prayers.

Regardless, I want to tell you something. God keeps working even when our marriages fall apart. God is working in my life now like never before. God is doing good things in my life every single day, and I hope the confidence that comes from him is evident to everyone I encounter. As a woman, I have never felt more loved and cherished than I do right now, and I am more sure than ever that God has a special place for me to fill in this world.

After my divorce, I continually tried to appreciate my new independent me and what God was doing in my life. I concentrated on God, my children and grandchildren, my work, my friends and my own health and fitness. God used that time to center me in him, calm my heart and teach me trust.

I was divorced about three years when my new husband came storming into my life. I really wasn't ready for a long-term, serious relationship when we met, but he was patient—and persistent. We have been married almost two years.

What I love most about him is that he wants first and foremost to be God's person—to continually discover and do God's will in his life. We share a spiritual bond that I never had in all my years with my first husband. We pray together, and that alone makes a huge difference. He has two great sons, two great daughters-in-law and three amazing grandchildren of his own. They have all given me an unbelievable welcome, and I'm impressed with the strong families they are building.

Not only is my husband trying to be God's person, but he also is intelligent and well-spoken and funny. He is comfortable in his own skin, and is not continually trying to readjust himself to make sure everyone likes him. And even though he can't sing very well (don't tell him that!) he sings to me all the time—opera, country western, blues, whatever. We laugh together. He is physically affectionate and has a generous heart. He also expects people to take responsibility for themselves.

Maybe I shouldn't mention this, but our love life is better than I ever thought possible, too. I know my children are probably cringing to read this! I only tell you this because when I was first divorced, I actually wondered if I could ever kiss another man. I couldn't picture myself even doing that, much less doing anything else. Boy was I wrong! My husband is more attuned to my needs and desires than I could have dreamed. I trust him, and I believe he would talk to me if he thought our relationship was not right, and we could do something about it. I can't fathom him sneaking off in the dark with another woman. I believe he is too honorable for that.

He's not perfect. Neither am I. We argue. He can be loud and opinionated. He can be unreasonable. He has a temper. I am hardheaded and like to make sure my side of the issue is heard. I can be argumentative. I like a fair exchange of ideas. I have a hard time with my checkbook. I lose things. I am not organized. He is a Democrat. I am a Republican. He is a Catholic. I am a non-denominational Christian. We disagree about things. But we always talk things out—face to face—even if it's very loud talking! If something is bothering me, he makes me look him in the face, and he says, "Talk to me." We talk until we work something out.

He cares about me and actually wants to know what I'm thinking. I care about him and want to hear his opinion. Even though we do not always agree, we always come to a mutually acceptable conclusion to the issue at hand. We are learning from each other, and we are stronger together than we could be on our own. I am thankful he is in my life. God is blessing us, and we are trying our best to figure out his plan for us, even though we have no idea where that will eventually take us.

Wherever it is, I have no doubt our life will be fulfilling and fun. My own day-to-day life as a woman is amazingly good, and I still pray that our children can be stronger because of what we have been through together. I want their lives to be full of all kinds of joy, gladness, and just plain fun. In a nutshell that's where my life is now.

I want you to know your life can be good, too—and not just if you get married again! God has fulfilling, joyful, fun plans for you—for unique, beautiful, competent you. Believe that and enjoy every single day he gives you to the fullest. Discover what amazing things he wants to do with you. Just remember, your best is yet to come!

LETTER TO MY COUNSELOR

I wrote my counselor after I had remarried, expressed thanks to her for her help and described my present life.

To My Counselor Barrie ...

In retrospect, those years were terrible to get through day to day, but the rewards that I'm reaping now are worth all of the pain. I learned much about God, about myself, about relationships, and about life. The lessons were not easy, but they were necessary to teach me certain things. Of course, I don't have all the answers, but I do have a renewed trust in the power of God to bring good to our lives even when we see nothing but sadness and heartache....

I have the peace of mind knowing I tried to bring good to my ex-husband's life. I am thankful for him because of our children, and because of that I wouldn't trade our relationship for anything.

But now, I can't believe I am having so much fun. A few years back I didn't think that was possible. It is like a huge weight has been lifted from my life, and you helped me make that transition. You kept saying it would happen, I just didn't quite believe you. Do you remember the day I asked you if anyone was ever really happy again after a divorce like this?

... I get calls almost every week from someone out there who is in the same position I was a few years back. I just hope my experiences can help make the journey easier for someone else.

... You'll always have a special place in my heart. Don't ever doubt the good you do.

Love,

Your Patient

SEVEN POEMS

They call it 'midlife crisis.'

Mild words for complete devastation.

Post Discovery

Our words are hard in the air ...

> *brittle,*
> > *strained,*
> > *imprisoned in stiff shells*
> > > *of doubt and fear.*

What I want
> *is the warmth*
> > *of a heartfelt laugh between us.*

Bored?

Have you seen my naked body so often
> *that you are no longer moved by it?*
Have you felt my bare skin so many times
> *that it's lost its power to excite?*
Are you bored with my shape
> *and with my familiar moves and sounds?*
Will I ever again
> *make you take a quick breath*
> > *of gratitude and joy?*

I wonder,
> *and I have to work hard*
> *not to be unbearably sad ...*
> *because I think I know the answer.*

Almost Perfect

Geese flying, honking overhead
Delicious cheese ravioli, leftover from last night
Two owls talking to each other in their own Morse code
Birds chattering everywhere
Perfect, breathless, 65 degree evening on the deck
The sun shining sideways through leaves—life-full green
A spring evening of perfection
*   listening to the game*
*   having a glass of wine*
Our youngest at a friend's
Our dog at my feet
A perfect evening … except
My husband loves another woman.

A woman who says her husband doesn't understand
*   and takes her children to counseling*
*   because they're having trouble in school*
*   and they aren't sleeping very well.*
For three years,
*   my husband has methodically, knowingly, callously*
*   destroyed our life.*
*   I'm incredibly inexpressibly sad.*

But I've got to face the truth.
I've got to make my heart face the reality that he wants to share
*   his life with someone else …*
*   and all my rage and tears won't change that.*
*   and thirty-three years of loving and living together*
*   won't change that.*

I've got to give up trying to make him understand
everything he's losing.
I've got to give up trying to make him see
everything he's destroying.
For one thing ... our grown up children
don't want to see the anguish
and the humiliation any longer.
It makes them sad
and angry,
and they wonder if they ever really knew their father at all.

My Life Partner

I feel so totally alone.
Who can understand this pain?
Who can understand the sense of agonizing disbelief
that my husband of 32 years would have so little care for me...
that he would have so little regard for my heart...
that he would have so little concern
about what this would do to me forever?
How is that possible?
Could I ever give my heart to a man like that again?
Could I ever feel safe with a man like that?
Could I ever entrust myself to a man who could do that for so long?
Who could look me in the eye
and lie
and betray my trust
with such selfish disregard ...
for so long?

Who could say to me,
*   "We could work this out*
*   if you weren't so unforgiving."*

And that very night
*   call her,*
*   and kiss her,*
*   and have her in his bed*
*   in Room 120 at the Fairfield Inn.*

Can We Mend?

How can our love survive
*   after your betrayal ...*
when you once again felt that intoxication,
*   that quickened heart,*
*   in moments stolen away*
*   in secret places*
*   with someone else?*
How can that ever, ever be mended ...
*   for me?*
*   or for you?*
How can you now be satisfied
*   with someone you grew tired of?*
*   someone you could so easily discard?*
*   someone whose heart you could tear apart*
*   without enough remorse*
*   to make you stop?*
How can I ever feel safe
*   that behind our loving*
*   you don't quietly wish*
*   you could be excited again?*

True Confessions

I'll admit
>*I want the security*
>>*that you want me completely*
>>>*without hesitation ...... nothing held back.*
>*I don't want to worry*
>>*that somewhere deep inside*
>>>*you feel like you*
>>>*had to give up the true 'love of your life'*
>>>>*for respectability.*

I'll admit
>*I want romance...*
>>*an extravagance of heartfelt affection.*
>*I want to know*
>>*that you have a tingling excitement*
>>>*about our future together.*

I'll admit
>*I want to live the rest of my life with a man*
>>*who loves me without reservation,*
>>*who is secure enough to show me that with fun*
>>>*and optimism*
>>>*and good-natured laughter.*
>*I want a man with a contented desire*
>>*to be honest and true...*
>*not someone who feels*
>>*hemmed in and restricted by faithfulness.*

I'll admit
>*I have doubts you can be that kind of man.*

I'll admit
>*I'm afraid you'll always think that*

money and things and activities
and being president of everything
will bring you satisfaction.
I'm afraid you will forever be looking
for something in the pages of Playboy and Penthouse
and between the legs of easy women
to fill the empty spaces you have inside.

I'll admit
I'm ready to say,
"Go ahead, have your cheap unbalanced immoral girlfriend."
I want someone better,
something richer,
a good life of love and laughter.
I'm tired
of hoping you'll grow up enough
to grasp the unbelievable pleasures
of love over the long run.
Or hoping you will learn to be content with what you have,
Or wishing you could understand the exquisite joys
of sharing your heart and your self
with me
and with your children and grandchildren.

I'll admit
most of all, I'm tired of your life of lies.

But you know what's really sad?

I'll admit
I keep wanting to give you another chance.
I keep thinking God will
somehow make this turn out all right.

I'll admit,
  after all these years,
    it's hard for me to give up on you ...
      and on us.

I'll admit
  it's hard for me to accept
    that it's time to let you go.

What Do You Think?

Did you actually think she was worth
  giving up your children every day?
Or that she could ever repair
  the quiet look of sadness in their eyes?
Did you really think she could take the place
  of seeing the family of geese with your grandchildren?
Or laughing around the table about "I eight the refrigerator?"
Did you really think she could fill up the empty spaces
  everywhere you turn?
Or could heal the hurt of people who loved you?
Or could soften the disappointment
  of people who respected you?
Did you really think she could replace
  the rich, deep pleasures of doing right?
You might have thought so ...
  or maybe still do.

But you're wrong.

Divorce

What an ugly
  caustic
    horrible word.

I hate how it looks on the page.

I hate the way it makes my heart hurt.

I hate the fears it conjures up...

  lonely nights
  with no one to feel close ... skin to skin
  lonely mornings
  with no one to look out the window
  while we're still snuggled under the sheets
  lonely days
  with no one to go for a quick bicycle ride

  going to soccer games alone
  going to school functions without you at my side
  holidays trips
    and I can't even imagine seeing you share life with someone else.

But when I can finally face the facts with less sadness,
maybe then I'll understand that divorce might mean something else.

Maybe it will mean
  nights when I'm totally secure that the important people in my life
    are honest
      and faithful.

maybe it will mean not having nights of knotted stomachs
  or mornings
    or middle of the afternoons

or feeling once again that sick,
gut-wrenching
discovery of betrayal.

Maybe it will mean looking out at the moon
and sharing the beautiful sight...
not wondering if you are somewhere screwing your girlfriend.

Maybe it will mean not agonizing in the darkness
wondering in the quiet if you wish
you were in someone else's bed.

Maybe it will mean feeling more free to be myself,
and sharing more time with people who laugh easily ...
people who are fun
and who know that God makes a difference.

Maybe it will mean finding bits of myself
that have somehow been lost over the years

and maybe finding someone good and true to share myself with.

Maybe.
But I still hate the word divorce,
and I'm utterly heartbroken it describes my life.

DISCUSSION GUIDE

FOR RADICAL WOMEN GROUPS

CHAPTER ONE
First, Survive

Theme Verse:

"Put your heart right, reach out to God—then face the world again –
firm and courageous, then all your troubles will fade from your memory
like floods that are past and remembered no more."

Job 11:13-15

1. What are your most pressing daily problems right now? Are you addressing those? If so, how? If not, what concrete steps can you take to address them?

2. Are you willing to reach out to God and face the world again? Are you taking care of yourself physically? How? If not, what can you do to begin taking care of yourself?

3. What is the single hardest thing for you to adjust to right now? Can you do anything about it? If so, what?

4. Where do you want to end up emotionally? Physically? Spiritually? What are you doing every day to get there? If nothing, what can you do?

5. Do you have someone—a friend, family member, friend from church or counselor—you can call any time during the day or night? If not, find someone. Most churches would be glad to help.

CHAPTER TWO
GET STRONG

Theme Verse:

"It is God who arms me with strength
And makes my way perfect."
2 Samuel 22:32

1. Do you consider yourself a strong woman? Why or Why not? Can a strong woman experience anger, sadness, and discouragement?

2. Describe a time in the past when you have demonstrated strength.

3. What does Jesus mean when he says, "My grace is sufficient for you, for my power is made perfect in weakness"? What does the Apostle Paul mean when he says, "Therefore will I boast all the more gladly about my weaknesses, so that Christ's power can rest on me. For when I am weak, then I am strong."? Are you letting God's power rest on you? How?

4. How can you best demonstrate and increase strength during this journey? Physically? Emotionally? Spiritually?

5. Can you accept your feelings of inadequacy and weakness for the moment and depend on God's strength and power to see you through this? How?

CHAPTER THREE
ORGANIZE THE CHAOS

Theme Verse:
"God hasn't invited us into a disorderly, unkempt life,
but into something holy and beautiful—
as beautiful on the inside as on the outside.

1 Thessalonians 4:7 (The Message)

1. What about this divorce is creating the most serious disruption in your life right now?

2. What physical and emotional clutter do you need to get out of your life? What steps can you take to start doing that?

3. Do you have a plan for getting your finances in order? If so, what is it? If not, where can you start?

4. Are you willing to make a conscious offering to God by donating to someone in need or to help a worthy cause? Will you have to give up something in order to do that?

5. Do you have your vital documents and papers in one spot where you can easily access them? Does a trusted person know where they are?

6. What are you doing to put new safety habits in place?

CHAPTER FOUR
Help Your Children

Theme Verse:
"He … established the law in Israel …
So the next generation would know them …
Then they would put their trust in God
And would not forget his deeds."
Psalm 78:5-7

1. Do you have a plan for the custody/living arrangements for your children still at home? Does it seem to be in their best interest? If you don't have a plan, what is the first step you need to take? Do your children have someone they can talk with about this situation other than you or your ex-husband?

2. What can you do to make this transition easier for your children? What would be a good first step or positive move in that regard?

3. Have you asked your children what they need from you? What did they say?

4. What do you want your ultimate spiritual statement to be to your children through all of this? Write it down and keep it in your thoughts every day.

5. Write down three positive things your children can learn from this experience.

CHAPTER FIVE
STAY CLOSE TO FAMILY AND FRIENDS

Theme Verse:
"And we know that all that happens
to us is working for our good
if we love God and are fitting into his plans."
Romans 8:28

1. How are your friends and extended family reacting to this situation? What behavior from you will gain their respect? What will make them lose respect for you?

2. What social groups are giving you support? What are you doing to maintain those connections? If you are losing touch with friends, what is one concrete thing you can do?

3. Have you found or started a positive divorce recovery group to share ideas and experiences with? Are they helping you move in the right direction? How? If you don't have a group, what can you do to change that?

4. Make a list of five good, happy, uplifting things you can talk about with your friends.

5. Write down an answer for friends you meet in the grocery store or at the post office who want to know what's going on. Frame the discussion positively if possible.

CHAPTER SIX
FACE REALITY

Theme Verse:

"For I know the plans I have for you, declares the Lord,
plans to prosper you and not to harm you,
plans to give you hope and a future."

Jeremiah 19:11

1. Have you fully accepted your situation and what it means for your future? What have you accepted? What are you having trouble accepting? How do you envision your future?

2. What are your biggest fears and worries about being divorced? Name three small actions you can take to address those fears.

3. Can you think of five positive things about being independent? Name them. What are positives about being out of your relationship with your ex-husband? Name them.

4. What are the strong points of the real you? Did your ex-husband encourage or discourage those attributes? Is there anything to keep you from developing them/building on them now?

5. What is something constructive you can do now that you felt inhibited about doing when you were married? What is one concrete step you can take to do that or develop that ability?

CHAPTER SEVEN
Choose to Change

Theme Verse:

*"Finally, brothers, whatever is true, whatever is noble,
whatever is right, whatever is pure, whatever is lovely,
whatever is admirable—if anything is excellent
or praiseworthy—think about such things."*

Philippians 4:8

1. Are you focusing on what can happen in the future, or are you still bound by what happened in the past? Name ways that you have learned to change your focus from the negative perceptions to positive realities.

2. Are you practicing ways to get fully into the moment?

3. List ten wonderful things about your life or yourself right now. How is your gratitude attitude?

4. Are you learning to appreciate nature for its own magnificence? Name specific ways you can do that.

5. Who is responsible for how your life turns out? What are specific ways you are learning to take control?

CHAPTER EIGHT
Embrace Transformation

Theme Verse:

*"Glory be to God who by His mighty power
within us is able to do far more than we would
even dare to ask or even dream of, infinitely beyond
our highest prayers, desires, thoughts or hopes."*

Ephesians 3:20

1. How are you doing on the forgiveness thing? What do you think is holding you up? What can you think of that will help you let go?

2. What could help you the most in getting started in the new life God has planned for you?

3. What is a specific thing you can do every day to give the situation and yourself completely to God?

4. What does this Radical promise from the book of Romans mean to you? "God is kind, but he's not soft. In kindness, He takes us by the hand and leads us to a radical life change." Do you really believe that? Is God leading you to a Radical new life? If so, how? If not, what can you do to move toward a new life?

5. What things are you specifically and consciously doing to help someone else? For this, anything counts. Being kind to the people you meet in your daily activities. Volunteering anywhere. Taking a grandchild to get an ice cream cone. Being a good listener.

6. Are you really taking that Radical step to believe God has an amazing new, abundant life for you? He promises it. Believe him! What one thing can you do right now to demonstrate your trust in God?

REFERENCES AND RESOURCES
By Chapter, in Order of Occurrence

Chapter One
First, Survive

Psalms 37:4 (NIV—New International Version)

Romans 13:14 (The Message)

Jeremiah 4:14 (NIV)

Psalms 51:7, 8, 10 (NIV)

Memoirs of a Geisha, Columbia Pictures Corporation, 2005.

Witness, Paramount Pictures, 1985.

Proverbs 17:22 (NIV)

Carol Hymnowitz, "Office Fashion Tip: Looking Grown Up Whatever Your Age," *Wall Street Journal*, Sept 13, 2005.

Psalms 118:24

Charles F. Horn, editor, *Great Men and Famous Women*, Vols. 1, 2, 3 (New York: Selmar Hess, Publisher, 1894).

Chapter Two
Get Strong

Shirley Wang and Betsy McKay, "More Reasons to Eat Your Veggies," *Wall Street Journal*, July 25, 2006.

Colossians 3:1 (The Message)

Aleksandr I. Solzhenitsyn, *The Gulag Archipelago* 1918-1956: *An Experiment in Literary Investigation* (Harper & Row, Harper Perennial Edition, 1991).

Azar Nafisi, *Reading Lolita in Tehran: A Memoir in Books* (New York: Random House, 2003).

Something's Gotta Give, Columbia Pictures Industries, Inc., and Warner Bros. Entertainment, Inc., 2003.

Psalms 18:32 (NIV)

Chapter Three
Organize the Chaos

Jeremiah 29:11-13 (NIV)

Chapter Four
Help Your Children

Bill Withers, "Lean on Me," sung by Bill Withers, from *Still Bill* (Sussex Records, 1971).
Ecclesiastes 4:9-10 (NIV)
Proverbs 20:7 (The Message)

Chapter Five
Stay Close to Family and Friends

1 Corinthians 5:11 (Living Bible)
Melissa Healy, "Life Support: Female friendship protects women's health, researchers say," *Kansas City Star*, July 5, 2005.
2 Corinthians 1: 3-4 (Living Bible)

Chapter Six
Face Reality

Nancy Gibbs, "MIDLIFE CRISIS? Bring It On!" *TIME*, May 16, 2005.
Carol Hymnowitz, "Women Often Discover Their Business Talent After Kids Are Raised," *Wall Street Journal*, June 15, 2005.

Chapter Seven
Choose to Change

John Boudreau, "IT'S ABOUT FORGIVENESS: When a relationship ends, making peace with the past may be the best thing to do," *Kansas City Star*, Oct. 20, 2003.
Fred Luskin, *Forgive for Good: A Proven Prescription for Health and Happiness* (San Francisco, Harper 2003).
David Maine, *The Preservationist* (New York: St. Martin's Press, 2004).
Jeffrey Zaslow, "Letting go of letting go: Society's formulas for grieving don't apply to everyone," *Kansas City Star*, Sept 13, 2005.
Juanita Goodvin and Suzy Sullivan, *Yes, This Day Is for Joy* (Wichita, Kan., Heart-Thoughts, Inc., 1989).
Abraham Harold Maslow, Richard Lowry, editor, *Toward a Psychology of Being* (Indianapolis, Ind.: John Wiley & Sons, Inc., Third Edition, 1999).
1 Corinthians 7:17 (The Message)

Chapter Eight
Embrace Transformation

Biblical passages about seeking and finding God:
Deuteronomy 4:9; Hebrews 11:6; James 4:8
Matthew 6:14, 15
Psalms 46:10
 Luke 6: 37, 38. (NIV)
Galatians 5:22, 23 (The Message)
Biblical Passages about not being afraid:
Isaiah 41:10; Psalms 46:1-2; Hebrews 13:5-6; 2 Timothy 1:7
1 Corinthians 7:11 (The Message)
Psalms 18:16-24. (The Message)

Notes

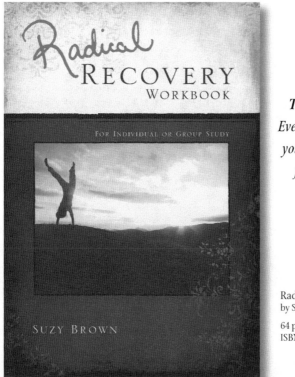